Towards the Lost Domain

Henri Alain-Fournier

Towards the Lost Domain: Letters from London, 1905

edited and translated by
W.J. Strachan

CARCANET

First published in Great Britain 1986 by
Carcanet Press Ltd
208–212 Corn Exchange Buildings
Manchester M4 3BQ
and 108 East 31st Street
New York, New York 10016

Letters courtesy of Alain Rivière, Editions Fayard,
Gallimard
Translation and editorial matter © copyright
W.J. Strachan 1986
All rights reserved
The publishers acknowledge the financial assistance of the
Arts Council of Great Britain

British Library Cataloguing in Publication Data

Alain-Fournier
   Towards the lost domain : letters from
   London 1905.
   1. Alain-Fournier —— Biography
   2. Novelists, French —— 20th century ——
   Biography
   I. Title   II. Strachan, W.J.
   843'.912   PQ2611.085Z/

ISBN 0-85635-674-3

Typesetting by Paragon Photoset, Aylesbury
Printed in England by SRP Ltd, Exeter

Contents

List of Illustrations

Introduction

On 2 July 1905, Henri Fournier, an eighteen-year-old school-boy, sailed from Dieppe to Newhaven. His aim — sternly reinforced by his schoolteacher parents — was to improve his English and to learn something about life in England. For the duration of his stay in London, coinciding with his school holidays, he was translator of correspondence at the factory of Sandersons, the wallpaper manufacturers. He returned to his home in La Chapelle-d'Angillon on 18 September.

Fournier's letters show him to be a born communicator, and from them his devotion to the idea of authorship already emerges. His observations on the English put him in the tradition of his countrymen such as Voltaire, Taine and Verlaine, who recorded their fascination with the contradictions in English manners and behaviour. But in Fournier's England there is no desperate East wind blowing, nor does he have Verlaine's cynicism — 'Perhaps it is good for one to live for a time among barbarians'. His reservations about the English and their ways are minimal, if downright.

Henri Fournier approached his trip to England in a spirit of adventure, characteristic of an adolescent who had entertained dreams of becoming a naval officer, and still had plans for exotic travel. He had been apprehensive about the impression he would make in his Paris interview with Mr Harold Sanderson, head of the firm; typically, he laid the ghost of his nervousness by drawing an imaginary caricature of the mutton-chopped chief. The interview had been arranged by M. Léon Bernard, Sanderson's Paris representative and the brother of one of Henri's schoolfriends, Jean Bernard. In the event, the outcome was satisfactory.

After he made the journey to London so enthusiastically described in his first letters home, a 'handsome' cab collected him at Victoria station and took him straight to the Sanderson factory at Heathfield Terrace, Turnham Green. The firm's secretary, Mr J. J. Nightingale, had agreed to take Fournier as a paying-guest in his home, 5 Brandenburgh Road (changed to 'Burlington' Road in the First World War), Gunnersbury. Thus two areas of interest — factory life and home life — were straightway open to an intelligent youth, already half in love with an England he knew only from books. In addition, London, with everything it could offer in the way of streets, parks, museums, concert-halls, was on his doorstep.

Henri explained to his parents the bargain struck: a slight reduction in his payment for board and lodging in exchange for French lessons he was to give Mr Nightingale. It was good news for his parents, whose salaries were stretched in financing his stay in London. Undoubtedly they hoped that their son's improved English would add considerably to his chances of gaining a place at the Ecole Normale Supérieure, and thus lead to a more prestigious teaching career than their own.

It also led to a fruitful relationship between Henri and his host. The Nightingales — who had two daughters: Clara, aged about eleven, and the two-year-old Florence — were a Non-conformist (Baptist) self-made couple in their early thirties, probably from Lancashire. Balzac's observation that 'Lancashire is the county where the women die for love' would not seem applicable to the matter-of-fact Mrs Nightingale. Either through thriftiness, or lack of imagination, or both, she failed to cater for the appetite of a healthy youth (with a gymnast's frame), energetically exploring London. Hence the complaints about hunger which Henri made to his parents (never to his hosts), and his *cri de coeur* on 13 July for breadrolls from home. Yet the Nightingales cannot have been too badly off. They had their income from their other paying guests, the two Martin sisters, who occupied the third floor above Henri. Mr Nightingale had a responsible job, acting as head of the firm during Mr Sanderson's frequent absences.

In his correspondence, Henri conveys his feelings about the couple with restraint towards Mrs Nightingale, and in glowing terms concerning her husband's generosity. At a later date, recalling his time in London in a letter to Jacques Rivière, he wrote:

8

Mr Nightingale, my English host, came to spend ten days in Paris, to my inexpressible delight. . . . Gently powerful, a very upright life. Like many English people, a poet without knowing it, a poet of the home, a poet of the countryside. . . . All Frenchmen seem trivial and petty to me, compared with this blond giant with an eagle's head who — except when he has decided to be a machine — is a *child*. In the central office of the factory . . . concentrating on understanding nothing outside his own function . . . making an effort not to reply when his wife makes hostile remarks. Standing there, silent, strong, but with a soul which disagreeable and hostile remarks apparently cannot penetrate . . .[1]

He also became attached to the suburb of Gunnersbury and its villas, with their coloured glass and lace curtains, and captivated by English parks. Two were within walking distance: Gunnersbury Park and Grove Park, Chiswick.

The Sanderson factory was not more than a couple of miles away to the north-east, at Turnham Green. It had an enlightened regime for the time: all employees were entitled to a week's summer holiday, the senior staff to two weeks, in addition to the usual public holidays. The firm ran a social club, 'Bleak House', which belied its name as, among other things, it was responsible for the annual party and ball. Henri's description of this occasion, with much space devoted to the children's activities, games and fancy-dresses, is a striking feature of the letter he wrote to Rivière on 23 July. We rightly recognize in this, and in his letter to his parents, the raw material he was later to transpose into a central theme of *Le Grand Meaulnes* — 'The Strange Fête' — half reality, half dream-world.

Despite his routine though not arduous work at the factory, Fournier found time to explore Edwardian London. The observations he recorded on paintings at the National Gallery show his visit was not a mere 'duty' one, like that to the National Portrait Gallery. They bear witness to an exceptional discernment. He picked out for special attention several paint-

[1] *Correspondance Alain-Fournier — Jacques Rivière* (Gallimard, 1926), vol. I, pp. 209–10.

ings then little known outside England. He was thrilled by Hogarth's *Shrimp Girl* — 'though only a sketch' — and by the Turners, especially *Rain, Steam, Speed*, which despite Ruskin's praise, was not as much admired as it is today.

It was, however, 'the collection of Mr Tate' that aroused his particular interest and curiosity. In France, until their satirical portrayal by Anatole France in *L'Ile des Pingouins* (1908), the Pre-Raphaelite Brotherhood had been more or less ignored. The work of Dante Gabriel Rossetti impressed Fournier most. Although an admirer of the French Symbolist painters and poets, he was taken aback by the symbolism in the vast canvases of George Frederick Watts, and had a shrewd comment to make on Millais' *Ophelia* — 'redeemed by a very Shakespearean peasant-girl's head'.

When it came to music, Fournier admitted his lack of competence to appreciate a programme at the Queen's Hall, and deferred to Rivière's expertise; his helpful comments arrived by return of post. The schoolboy friendship of these two almost exact contemporaries began at the Lycée Lakanal, and continued throughout their lives. Their bond of affection transcends differences of background and social status, of which the Rivière parents were hyper-conscious. This was especially true of Jacques' father, a distinguished medical doctor in Bordeaux, who looked down on the teaching profession of the Fourniers. Indeed when Jacques fell in love with Henri's sister Isabelle, they had to keep their engagement secret for a time and the Rivières absented themselves from the wedding ceremony at Saint-Germain-des-Prés. The marriage consolidated the friendship of Jacques and Henri, who had kept in touch by voluminous correspondence when separated, first during Henri's London stay, then through periods of military service. Their reunion during the summer of 1907 at Cenon (Bordeaux), at the home of Rivière's maternal grandparents, was a great occasion for exchanges of views and shared enthusiasms. It was a disappointment to both that the poet Francis Jammes, whom they admired, had to put off their visit to him at home in Orthez. Henri must have found some consolation in continued relations with the painter and art-critic André Lhote, another Bordelais, whom he found occasion to meet when the painter came to Paris and with whom he maintained a long correspondence.[1]

The facts are set out in the accompanying Chronology — 'a shilling life will give you all the facts' — but it requires a sympathetic reading of the letters that passed between Rivière and Fournier to understand the importance and depth of their friendship. It was based on shared interests, despite the differences of opinion that give the edge to their correspondence. Their tastes in 1905 were adolescently eclectic: they could enjoy the Symbolist poets, revel in Maeterlinck's *Pelléas et Mélisande* set to Debussy's music, and at the same time admire Verhaeren's realism expressed in *vers libres*. A glance at their biographies shows how their tastes and talents developed and matured: Fournier more in the creative, Rivière in the critical field.[2]

It is therefore the more significant that it was Rivière's criticism, both positive and negative, of Fournier's poem 'A travers les étés' — the subject of their discussion in the present volume (see pp. 178–82) — that helped shape his friend's future writing. Rivière is encouraging, for example, in his praise of the long evocation of Nançay (see pp. 98–101). On the other hand, he warns against the dangers of Dickensian sentimentality, bordering on the mawkish.

Fournier's piece on what was to become 'Le Vieux Nançay' in *Le Grand Meaulnes*, when he admits to be 'indulging in literature', and his account of the burglary at 5 Brandenburgh Road, demonstrate how effectively he can tailor his style to suit the theme. They also show, no less importantly for our understanding of Fournier's personality, how he could live simultaneously in two worlds. This dichotomy pervades his letters: concern for his long-term ambition as a writer on the one hand, and an all-too-pressing anxiety (shared with Rivière) about examinations on the other. Can two more promising talents — one a potential novelist of genius, the other future editor of the *Nouvelle Revue française* — ever have been

[1] The present writer had many conversations with Simone Lhote particularly, after her husband's death, about the importance of Alain-Fournier in his life in Bordeaux and Paris.

[2] For full information about his life and career see 'Jacques Rivière et les Lettres Françaises 1886–1925', Bordeaux, Exposition à la Bibliothèque Municipale, 19 novembre–31 décembre 1977.

11

judged academically inadequate by the Ecole Normale Supérieure in successive years?

In Fournier's case there was a further complication: how to cope with his obsession with the 'demoiselle' he had encountered in Paris. As he was leaving an exhibition at the Grand Palias on 1 June 1905, he saw a beautiful blonde girl, accompanied by a bent old lady, and was so attracted by her demeanour that he followed them along the Cours-la-Reine and on to the *bateau-mouche* they boarded, disembarked with them and proceeded to the Boulevard Saint-Germain, where they disappeared into a house. She had looked at him twice. Fascinated by her 'pure' beauty, slender figure, blue eyes, he returned to wait under her window whenever he could get away from the Lycée Lakanal. On 10 July, in a terrific downpour, he saw her raise a corner of the curtain at her window. She was dressed in black and had a book in her hand. She smiled to find him there again.

The following morning, Whit Sunday, wearing his uniform so that she should know he was a schoolboy, Fournier suddenly met her face to face in the street: he said 'You are beautiful', but she passed on without heeding him. Later in the day he followed her to mass at Saint-Germain-des-Prés, and he seized the opportunity to ask her forgiveness; 'You haven't annoyed me,' she replied. 'You have behaved very respectfully. I bear you no ill-will . . . I forgive you.' She even gave him her name, Yvonne de Quiévrecourt, and said that her father was a naval officer in Toulon. Fournier wrote later to his friend Bichet that she spoke with a slight stress on each syllable, and on the 'b' of 'bon' as she said, 'A quoi bon?' (What's the use?). ' "We are two children; we have behaved foolishly." Much further on, she turned round, stood stock still and looked towards me before disappearing forever.'

The experience made the deepest mark on him; it had to be lived through and worked out in his poems and prose writings. We only have glimpses of this obsession in the London letters, and his dejection rarely surfaces in his buoyant and often humorous correspondence. The loneliness he talks about to Rivière (13 August) is partly caused by the house being temporarily empty, but he confesses that 'it adds up to a very tender and deep emotion which could be called "nostalgia for the past" '. This emotion was to haunt him for the rest of his life. His thoughts were never far distant from the region of his childhood and youth, and never ceased to return — even when she was lost to him in marriage — to the creature 'of the slenderness and elegance . . . beyond all dreams' (17 June 1905; see appendix II).

In his 9 July letter to Rivière, Fournier voices two themes that occur in his life and in the novel: the minor and temporary hankering after a naval career, and the abiding one for Yvonne de Quiévrecourt (de Galais in *Le Grand Meaulnes*). 'I would like to . . . talk to you about HER whose face suddenly . . . reappeared the other evening with such awesome clarity that it stirred me to the depths of my being. . .'. He devoted a whole poem, written during his English stay, to the development of the theme involving Yvonne as the imaginary châtelaine of an idealized château. I have mentioned the Sanderson's annual garden-party and ball, from which even a detail such as the 'directoire' hats of the English girls is transferred to a French setting and used in his novel. His letters are scattered with observations and ideas that are developed in *Le Grand Meaulnes*: a considerable part of his 13 August letter is devoted to uncle Florent, who lived in the Sologne at Nançay, and who is lifted as Uncle Florentin — along with his family and his store — almost unchanged into Chapter 2, Part III of *Le Grand Meaulnes*. Henri's own cousin, Marie-Rose, re-emerges as Marie-Louise, 'folding lengths of cloth' in her father's store. The reader interested in such transpositions will find other examples. The one I find particularly touching is contained in the same letter of 13 August, where Fournier writes: 'What I mean by a dream is a vision that is beginning to fade, of an afternoon as it encounters the dazzling white of a sunshade'. It is taken up again in his poem 'A travers les étés', in *Le Grand Meaulnes* (Chapter 15, Part I), in a long note written to himself during his English stay — 'when shall I rediscover her slight figure that afternoon when she stood facing me in her brown dress and parasol . . .' — and in a subsequent letter addressed to the real Yvonne after her marriage (see appendix II).

Such a dwelling on a highly romanticized past, which might be considered morbid once adolescence is left behind, was essential to Alain-Fournier's creative process. In this and in his search for the perfect love, Fournier is on similar ground to that of his contemporary, Marcel Proust, whose *Du côté de chez Swann* was published in the same year (1913) as *Le Grand Meaulnes*. The novels share a boy's perspective on events, the theme of inaccessible love, and devotion to village life — in, respectively Combray and 'le Vieux Nançay'.

The perspective, though, was something Fournier had learnt from Dickens, as he mentions in his London letters. Shortly after his return to France, he began to read Thomas Hardy, and *Tess of the D'Urbervilles* and *Jude the Obscure* had a profound effect on him. Furthermore, he adopted a treatment of territorial nomenclature — a mixture of real and fictional names — based on that for the region he was to use as the setting for *Le Grand Meaulnes*, with which he was as familiar as Hardy was with his Wessex.[1]

Such concerns are already evident in the letters of the embryonic novelist. But for the most part his energies are devoted to observation of the English scene, whether listening to hell-fire preachers in the street or the notions Mr Nightingale voiced from his rocking-chair. Fournier talks politics with his host and literature with the teachers in the house; his reading embraces Kipling and Wells. England, her inhabitants and language, had captivated him, and it was a fascination that lasted.

[1] For further remarks on Fournier's reading, and on the parallels with Hardy in particular, see the present writer's article in *PN Review* (Manchester), vol.13, no.4.

Translator's Note

In view of the sad and untimely death in 1983 of Christopher Hewett, founder of the Taranman Gallery and Press — who conceived and planned the present work, which he invited me to translate — it seemed appropriate to say something about the genesis and development of the project. He loved *Le Grand Meaulnes*, Alain-Fournier's masterpiece, to which I had introduced him during his schooldays at Bishop's Stortford College. He had an empathy for its author that dissolved the time between the book's publication in 1913, and his obsession forty-five years later with the novel and its mystique.

He shared Fournier's predilection for the 'romantics', the *poètes maudits*: Verlaine, Rimbaud, and above all the poems and novels of Gérard de Nerval. Hewett quotes him in a notebook written during his army service in Cyprus: 'Ils reviendront, ces Dieux que tu pleures toujours! Le temps va ramener l'ordre des anciens jours . . .'; he adds, from James Joyce, 'Corpus Domini Nostri, could it be? Another life, a life of grace and virtue and happiness. It was true. It was not a dream from which he would wake . . .'. Further, he wrote to me during this Cyprus period, 'I have just read *Le Grand Meaulnes* for the fourth time.'

It is not surprising, therefore, that in the summer of his last year at the Ruskin School of Drawing at Oxford, he should go on a cycling tour of France with the particular aim of exploring the Sologne and parts of Berry associated with *Le Grand Meaulnes*. I quote from a letter he wrote to me, dated 11 August 1959:

La Chapelle d'Angillon: 'le jardin de l'Archevêque' at Bourges where Frantz de Galais met Valentine — . . . these I have seen: Epineuil-le-Fleuriel on my return from Avignon. A little way from the village lives one who went to school with Fournier — M. Vincent. 'Could I make a drawing?' He was flattered.

Loroy: I grew friendly with one of the villagers — Mme Rocher. At dusk we sat outside on straw chairs . . . She gave me flowers from her garden, but this flower, for what it is worth, comes from 'the Lost Domain' — Loroy with woods — their still impenetrable green and ivy-mantled Gothic arches reminiscent of Nerval's Chantis . . .

It was not until 1975 that Hewett and I followed the same trail by car — to Bourges, through the Sologne country with its brackish ponds and fir-woods, spending a day and night at La Chapelle-d'Angillon (La Ferté-d'Angillon of the novel), where Alain-Fournier's name can be seen on the 1914–1918 War Memorial in the parish church.

Despite Hewett's preoccupation with the Taranman Gallery from 1974, the memories renewed by the tour led him to carry out researches in the Alain-Fournier archives, made possible by the willing and indispensable co-operation of Alain Rivière, Fournier's nephew, representing the Fournier Estate.

Some of Fournier's letters, including fourteen communications — three of them postcards — from England to his family, had already been published by Emile Paul in *Lettres d'Alain-Fournier à sa famille* (Paris, 1949), but Hewett discovered that a number of letters and postcards of the London period had not been published. With some excitement he found that seven of the letters in the Emile Paul book were incomplete, and he set about restoring these considerable omissions — some existed only in manuscript — which throw further light on his relations with his family during that time in London.

Hewett's idea of including several important letters to Fournier from Jacques Rivière was inspired, since the dialogue between these fellow-pupils from the Lycée Lakanal is uninhibited, and revealing about their contrasting personalities.

The letters in the appendices, written above all for himself to release almost unbearable emotions, are the unguarded, spontaneous outpourings of a Fournier obsessed with the image and memory of his brief encounters with Yvonne de Quiévrecourt in June 1905. Such intimate, almost embarrassing declarations are in strong contrast with the passages in his correspondence which he light-heartedly describes as 'literature'. It seemed, however, important to include them for the light they throw on Fournier's 'grande passion', the feelings attendant on which are the *sine qua non* and inspiration of *Le Grand Meaulnes*.

Acknowledgements

My thanks are due first and foremost to Christopher Hewett's sisters, Stella Saludes and Beryl Bjelke, for giving the project their warm support and blessing, and for their assistance in arranging for the book to be taken on by Carcanet Press. They rightly regard it as an important memorial to their brother, a feeling I naturally share.

The great help Alain Rivière gave Hewett has already been mentioned. I should add my gratitude for his replies to my queries, and especially for allowing me to quote from the *Catalogue de l'Exposition Jacques Rivière et les Lettres Françaises, 1886–1925*, held at the Bibliothèque Municipale de Bordeaux in 1977. That and the booklet *Séjour à Londres et influences anglaises dans l'oeuvre d'Alain-Fournier*, and the *Catalogue de l'exposition aux pays d'Alain-Fournier* (containing the full text of the poem 'A travers les étés'), both published by the Association des Amis de Jacques Rivière et d'Alain-Fournier, which Alain Rivière also supplied, have been invaluable.

My friend and ex-colleague Germaine Castaing-Jones helped me over knotty problems in many long sessions. I am also indebted to my former pupil Reg Powell for topographical research; to Giles Barber, Librarian of the Taylor Institution, Oxford, for pinpointing the Fournier correspondence concerning the Nightingales' visit to Paris, quoted in *Alain-Fournier et son Oeuvre* (Hachette, 1968) by Jean Loize in a passage the latter sent to Hewett, and for photocopying Colette's story 'Nonoche', published in the *Mercure de France*.

Others who have helped me include Cecily Mackworth, Mallarmé expert, with her translation of the lines quoted by Rivière (20 September 1905); Denis Fielder, with some nomenclature in the 'Notes on Wagner'; Stuart Barr, who supplied answers to some source queries; David Arkell, who generously advised concerning Fournier's postcards; Angelina

Bacon, Research Assistant at the National Gallery for information concerning *The Rape of the Sabine Women*; Jean Loize, for information about the Benoist family; to the London Museum and to Philip Philo, curator of Gunnersbury Park Museum, for information about the Rothschilds' park; Victoria Burnell of the Tate Gallery, who replied to queries about the correct titles of paintings mentioned by Fournier. I should add that anyone writing about Fournier must be indebted in one way or another to Robert Gibson's informative biography of Fournier, *The Land without a Name* (London, 1975). The French publishers, Gallimard, who took over from Emile Paul, kindly authorized the use of material translated from the latter's collection. With so much co-operation on every side before and during my work on the project, I must apologize for any names inadvertently omitted. The *Daily Telegraph* Information Bureau came to my rescue over some London topography of 1905.

Finally, my gratitude goes to Michael Schmidt of Carcanet, for his part in saving the whole project from oblivion, and managing to time its production for the centenary year of Fournier's birth; and to his colleague, Robyn Marsack, for her skilful editing and her suggestions regarding the arrangement of the text, choice of illustration, and not least, her enthusiasm for the material.

Chronology

1886	3 October	Henri Alban Fournier born to Marie Albanie Fournier (neé Barthe) and Sylvain Baptiste Augustin Fournier, schoolteachers in La Chapelle-d'Angillon.
1889	11 July	Birth of Isabelle Fournier.
1891		M. Fournier appointed to school at Epineuil-le-Fleuriel.
1898	October	Henri enters the Lycée Voltaire, Paris.
1901	30 September	Enters the Lycée at Brest to prepare for admission to the naval training-ship *Borda*.
1903	January	Transfers to the Lycée at Bourges (now named after him).
	July	Obtains his Baccalauréat.
	October	Enters the Lycée Lakanal at Sceaux, south of Paris. Meets Jacques Rivière (b. 1886 in Bordeaux).
1904–1905		Working for the entrance examination to the Ecole Normale Supérieure (ENS), training college for the top echelon of teachers.
1905	1 June	First encounter with 'la belle inconnue', Yvonne de Quiévrecourt (see introduction and appendices).
	2 July	Departs for England to work for Sandersons as their French clerk. Lodges with the Nightingale family.
	17 September	Returns to La Chapelle-d'Angillon, via Paris and Bourges. Meanwhile Rivière has failed the entrance to the ENS, but receives a bursary to the university at Bordeaux.
	1 October	Henri returns to Lakanal; reading includes Hardy's novels.
1906	June	Rivière begins his army service. Henri sits written papers for ENS entrance, which he fails.
	October	Henri's grandmother, 'Maman Barthe', moves to Paris to housekeep for Henri, now a day pupil at the Lycée Louis-le-Grand, and Isabelle, at the Lycée Fénelon.
	17 October	Yvonne de Quiévrecourt marries a naval doctor, Brochet.
	14 November	Death of grandmother Fournier, at Nançay.
1907	April	Rivière released from military service, joins Henri in

		Paris and meets Isabelle and Maman Barthe for the first time.
	24 July	Henri, having passed the written section of the ENS entrance examination, fails the oral test.
	25 July	He learns that Yvonne de Quiévrecourt is married. 'She's gone away. I am all alone.'
	August	Spends a fortnight with Rivière at his maternal grand-parents' villa in Cenon. They intend to cycle over to see Francis Jammes, but the poet is away.
	September	Rivière stays with the Fourniers at La Chapelle.
	2 October	Henri begins his military service as a dragoon, but at his request is soon transferred to the infantry.
	2 December	Rivière and Isabelle secretly engaged; the Rivières disapproved of the Fourniers.
	25 December	Publication of the essay 'Le Corps de la Femme' in *La Grande Revue*, under the name 'Alain-Fournier' (another Henri Fournier was a famous racing cyclist).
1908	February	The Fourniers move to Paris, M. Fournier to teach at Vincennes and Mme Fournier at Bagnolet.
	26 February	Announcement of Isabelle's engagement.
	October	Henri now a sergeant, training to be an officer. Rivière meets André Gide for the first time.
1909	March	Rivière submits Henri's 'La Partie de plaisir' to Gide for the *Nouvelle Revue française (NRF)*; it is rejected.
	April	Henri's last six months of service are spent in Mirande, south-west France. Major religious crisis.
	July	Henri fails the English *licence* examination, and Rivière fails in the Philosophy *agrégation* examinations.
	24 August	Wedding of Rivière and Isabelle Fournier in St Germain-des-Prés (where Henri had seen Yvonne praying four years previously).
	September	He learns that Yvonne Brochet has had a son.
	25 September	Henri demobilised; goes to live in his parents' Paris flat, along with the Rivières.
	November	Rivière's 'Introduction à une métaphysique du rêve' published in the *NRF*.
1910	January	Fournier's 'L'Amour cherche les lieux abandonnés' published in *L'Occident*.
	February	Meets Jeanne Bruneau — Annette in his correspondence — the original of 'Valentine' in *Le Grand Meaulnes*.
	May	Joins the staff of *Paris-Journal*, for which he writes a regular literary column.
	10 August	'Le Miracles des trois dames de village' published in *La Grand Revue*.

	October	Gives private French lessons: one pupil is T.S. Eliot, whom he introduces to Rivière.
		Meets Charles Péguy.
1911	25 March	'Le Miracle de la fermière' published in *La Grande Revue*.
	23 August	Difficult birth of his god-daughter, Jacqueline Rivière.
	September	'Portrait' published in *NRF*.
	December	Rivière appointed secretary of the *NRF*.
1912	April	Henri becomes secretary to Claude Casimir-Perier; becomes interested in his employer's wife, the actress Simone.
	20 December	Death of René Bichet.
1913		Fournier finishes writing *Le Grand Meaulnes*.
	May	Goes to Rochefort and meets Yvonne de Quiévrecourt. He hands her the unposted letter of September 1912 (see Appendix).
	June	Begins his affair with Simone Casimir-Perier.
	July	*NRF* serializes *Le Grand Meaulnes*.
	November	It is published in book form by Emile-Paul, and narrowly misses winning the Prix Goncourt.
1914		Simone and Henri decide to collaborate on a play, as her husband no longer needs a secretary. They spend two months in Trie.
	July	They lunch in Bordeaux with the Rivières; it is the last time the latter see Henri.
	1 August	Henri is called up as lieutenant; Simone and his parents follow him as far as Auch.
	12 August	The regiment departs for the front.
	22 September	Fournier reported missing after a reconnaissance patrol on the Meuse Heights. His body was never recovered; his name may be found on the war memorial in the church at La Chapelle.
1925	14 February	Death of Jacques Rivière, of typhoid fever.

19 June 1905   *Sceaux*

My dear Parents,

I was waiting for the result of the interview with the English people, I am therefore obliged to send this promised letter before receiving the verdict.[1] I'm too exhausted by the heat and my gymnastics to enlarge on what little news I have.

As far as Paris is concerned, I have scarcely any, and indeed why should I, now that I am styled a servant of a large firm? The day before yesterday, among the witty extravagancies he let drop, Monsieur Bernard expressed his eagerness to talk about the past when 'he hadn't the nerve to call on you'.

As for England, I am still waiting: Mr Sanderson came yesterday, and Jean is to write to me immediately. I may receive a message any time from this evening. Mr Sanderson has been described to me as a phlegmatic and very *matter-of-fact* Englishman. I'm very much afraid that all Monsieur Bernard's eloquence will not succeed in softening him. It so happens that I received a letter today from Monsieur Lavaron, but his items of information cannot (I presume) be of any use to me since they are all about houses, boarding-houses where you can pay by the month or months. I'll thank him in the course of the next few days, and that will take care of that.

I have met the poet and winner of the Sully-Prudhomme competition of 1903, Charles Dumas.[2] I dined with him and spent Tuesday afternoon in his company. He is about to publish a play he is now working on. He is a charming young man, and I passed a quiet and most agreeable evening with him. Although he is usually nervous and quiet, he stayed almost four hours just chatting to me in the drawing-room, asking questions, discussing things in general. I'm told he found me very congenial. Friendly relations are invariably mutual. I expect to be seeing him again. (Long hair, rather too 1830, eyes rather too 1830, refined features, good head, dandyish suit. My caricature is a pretty good likeness.)[3]

I went along with friends to two salons recently and on Wednesday afternoon, the day before the exam — for some — I had lunch in the country at Noisy-le-Sec.[4] On Sunday — and I noticed that Monsieur Bernard was appreciative — I accompanied Jean to the Grand Cycling Championship — small but not insignificant expenses! Not to mention the pleasant surprise the boy reserved for me on Saturday, when he told me that the laundry-woman wouldn't be ready until Sunday which left me without a collar and cuffs to wear! Not to mention either the laundry I had to pay for all the same when I got back, my subscriptions, the trip (seat etc.) with Monsieur Meur[5] to Port Royal, the unexpected levy for the school photograph album (with us in it — for the library). Nor, finally, am I mentioning all the current expenses that make the hair of my poor purse stand on end anyway, despite the sensible and vigorous opposition it puts up, and empties it of its ten francs.

In the country the other day, I thought about your cherries which must be starting to redden. Lucky you!

I'm getting bored here. It's stifling . . . I am knocked out by the heat I adore and gymnastics that I adore no less. If I'm not awarded the second prize this year, there's no justice in heaven. My great, unbeatable record consists in executing the most difficult feats in the most correct gear and without a crease out of place. On test days, the impeccable, classic and elegant way I climb the rope and move across the rings four times in succession and do my trapeze act, is acclaimed with a unanimous voice, or rather murmur, of admiration.

On this portrayal of myself, upside down and muscular, I hug you with all the strength I can muster.

Henri

P.S. Thank Mother for her long letter.

Thank you for the stamps. I'm not pressing the Richefeu business. My suit is going to cost 62 francs. I think the material is attractive. The pattern is in my room, I'll send it on to you. Thanks.

1 Fournier was interviewed in Paris by Mr Harold Sanderson, head of the famous British wallpaper firm. The connection had been initiated through Jean Bernard, a school-friend.
2 Sully-Prudhomme competition, founded in honour of the poet of that name, one of the chief contributors to the anthologies *Parnasse contemporain* (1866–76).
3 Fournier sometimes illustrated his letters with amusing, often self-mocking, sketches. In this he drew a caricature of Charles Dumas, poet and playwright.
4 Where the Bernard family lived.
5 History teacher at the Lycée Lakanal, Fournier's school in Paris.

2 TO MARIE AND AUGUSTE FOURNIER

3 July 1905   *London*

My dears,

On a small table, under a large garden sunshade, in the calm and freshness of all the houses that surround me, I'm going to try and describe my journey and arrival as briefly, yet as fully as possible.

From Paris, Gare Saint-Lazare, to Dieppe, I'm content to read through the letters of recommendation with which my pockets are crammed. It is night. I am beginning to get the feel of England in my own way, that is, of seeing it in the person of an English farmer and his wife and a *little darling*, and from what I've read about England and from *David Copperfield* in particular. It was expressed in an altogether strange and touching way. The two London workmen at the far end of the compartment, grotesque in their poverty and giving vent to their feelings in violent and spasmodic utterances, complete the picture.

Dieppe — half-past twelve — a provincial town, still lit up in some areas. Dismal squares that evoke memories of every depressing town you've ever set eyes on or imagined and must look equally grim at this hour of night. The train takes us through it all and straight to the boat.

It is an English boat, and this is where the foreigner's real impression begins. Two boys shout something about our descending to the lower deck — which I don't at first understand. Even on this small boat, the emigrants' deck presents a moving sight. Every kind of picturesque poverty, Italian or Chinese, grotesque poverty that doesn't give a damn, tying up its baggage, depositing it on the seats and sitting on it, poverty that cocks a snook at the official who is asking everybody's name and nationality, tender and moving poverty, husbands and wives falling asleep, locked in each other's arms.

Departure of the boat after two terrifying blasts from the siren, the usual cries of anguish and loneliness. Passengers stump round the deck, weaving their way through groups of people and piles of luggage.

Finally, the sea, the open sea. A ship, lit up, disappears. Sea all round, brown, black with grey waves moving and merging into the uniformly pale tones of a sky with only a few stars. For a moment, the ship, lighted and far off, reminds me of certain Whistler canvases that consist of one vast symphony of twilight greys.

The crossing takes five hours. I'm overcome with sleepiness, I'm no sooner seated than I doze off for an hour, huddled up in my overcoat, with my head drooping. — (Oh dear! I'm going to have to cut this short: Mrs (Missize) Nightingale has just asked me to accompany her with her lady friend to Covent Garden.) In my next, I'll pick up the thread at this point.

All you need to know now is that on arriving safe into port, and in the boss's absence, I came upon the chief secretary who immediately suggested that over and above my agreed work, we should study English together, offered me a room in his house, but on trial only, because he thinks it too small (otherwise they wouldn't be able to board me for less than 20 shillings; I'll certainly try to accept), gave me lunch with himself, his wife and their two *babies*[1] — today an odd lunch — set me free this evening in this delightful, fresh and green quarter of London where the notes of a piano reach me and it seems as if my life is beginning all over again and I am going to start out with Miss Nightingale to the public school in full sunlight.

I am managing marvellously well with my English.

Kisses,

Henri

My address: Mr Henri Fournier, at Mr Nightingale's, 5 Brandenburgh Road, Chiswick, LONDON.

1 Clara, aged eleven, and Florence, aged two.

3 TO MMS RIVIÈRE, GUINLE, GUÉNIFFEY, CHESNEAU, BICHET, CHOTARD, GAZANNOIS AND CO.

[postmarked] 5 July 1905   *Chiswick*

'I'm not missing either Lakanal or you although you are nice chaps, I'll soon be writing to young Rivière without waiting for a reply.'

On a postcard of Holloway Castle, with the text in quotes.

8 July 1905   *London*

My dear little Isabelle,

I'm very much afraid you have not received my last letter, as the address was not at all right. I had quite forgotten the number of the regiment and I had written *route de Moulins* instead of *route de Limoges*. However I hope the letter will arrive, or is arrived, because it seems to me that «Mr Brusseau maître sellier» is sufficient. I'm not sure, alas — I'm anxiously expecting your answer and, when received, I shall give my parents closed letter that they will hand you. Excuse, please, the postcard. Kiss for me Miss Reine and Miss Jeanne.

My best Kisses for you, darling.   *Henri*

This postcard was written in English.

9 July 1905   *London*

My dear Parents,

Sunday evening. It has been raining. From my bedroom I can smell the freshness rising from the lawns and chestnut-trees. I'm hurrying to write this to you before dark.

JOURNEY'S END. From Dieppe to Newhaven between midnight and six o'clock in the morning. Heavy slumber on a deck seat, punctuated hourly by a thirty-minute turn in the keen morning air, with the whole sky and the sea gradually turning white. At daybreak, a destroyer passes on the horizon. Return of the old yearning to become a sailor; but it fades away, and at six o'clock the distant view of the white chalk cliffs of Albion (Albus = white). Newhaven — my first conversations in English over changing a little money, customs' inspection of my luggage, etc.

Then from Newhaven to London, endless fields and

meadows, trees, everything of an unforgettable brilliant green!

London — vast — with its huge bridges across the broad Thames, roofs below the level of the train, an infinity of roofs, clean, bright, symmetrical. London with all its greenness, parks, gardens, its clean, busy streets, its shops bright and prosperous — its impressive policemen, and soon, suburban London with its houses, each of which is a miracle: you feel the urge to stop and examine each one individually, at leisure, and there are so many of them. Just like the little 'châteaux of Vieux Nançay',[1] minus the turrets: with small but solid well-polished front doors, bricks of exquisite tones, windows of coloured glass and lace curtains. Foliage everywhere, the notes of piano and flute rising up on every side.

And this is where I'm living at present. In a tiny bedroom on the second floor in one of these houses.

MY DUTIES. They're not yet finally settled. Mr Nightingale who is the secretary and, next to Mr Sanderson, the head of the firm, has not only made me responsible for the postal service — which is rather boring — but every morning I'm given, in addition, letters to file. The rest of the time I'm handed bundles of letters from which I extract my notes on commercial English.

Now and then I'm aware of someone putting the odd letter down beside me for me to translate from English into French or vice versa, always with the same message pinned to it: 'M. Henri Fournier. Kindly write the attached in French and return to me. J.N.'

I think one of two things is going to happen, either I shall replace the young man who sees to the post and is leaving tomorrow, or they will put me in with the young staff of both sexes who translate the letters. The former alternative is more likely since otherwise there would be nobody to do the job.

So, for the first few days, without a dictionary and naturally at full speed, I translated some of these commercial letters, terrifyingly concise and exact. These were immediately poly-copied and despatched — an error might involve grave con-sequences — in a commercial jargon which is as unfamiliar to me in French as it is in English.

I did this with superb aplomb, but it was with a slight misgiving as I returned each letter. It was thanks to the comments of some of the office-girls on words I didn't know that I got by. I now own a dictionary but it is of little use for business correspondence.

The fact remains that at the end of this week, that is on *Saturday at half-past twelve*, when I'd done nothing on Monday, hardly translated twenty letters and handled ten files the rest of the week — although the sum agreed was 8 shillings a week, someone went past me and all the other employees and put down beside me without my noticing it, 10 shillings in the little packet I enclose. That was nice, wasn't it?

I remember papa relating how eager grandpa Fournier was to set eyes on his first money order. That's why I am sending him this little packet which contained the first money I have ever earned. It is odd that it should have been in a factory. Still odder that I should owe it to my knowledge of English.

MY LODGINGS AND MY HOSTS. I am able to add, furthermore, that I've gained much more than that this week. In fact, Mr Nightingale, after I'd spent Monday at his house and heard his replies to the questions I put to him, told me I should have a problem finding board and lodging for *15* shillings a week even in an indifferent boarding-house. He also remarked that two ladies who live in two rooms on the first floor of their house, pay 30 shillings each just for the room.[2] He informed me finally that food and keep in a 'respectable establishment' was excessively dear. Having said that he offers me, for a trial period of two weeks — since they don't know how it will work out — board and lodging for 12 shillings a week on condition I give him a French lesson every evening from 7 to 8. He could hardly be kinder.

This week, that is to say yesterday evening, I only gave him 10 shillings — exactly what I had earned, and so I haven't cost you a penny. So you see that my knowledge of English brings me in more than 10 shillings.

Every evening I sit in a rocking-chair next to Mr Nightingale and give him his French lesson. He is an extraordinarily well-built man, young-looking, fair-skinned and handsome and smokes a pipe. Although amazingly obstinate and overpowering, he is exceedingly kind to everybody and plays the fool with his wife and children.

His wife — turned-up nose. His small daughter — Miss Clara Nightingale: turned-up nose. Baby Florence — turned-

up nose. And all three, *like all English females*, in long dresses, far too loose-fitting and uncorsetted. It makes them look, at first sight, I can't say why, somehow bundled up. Very boyish nevertheless. Cycling mad and seeming totally unaware that they are girls and that young men exist. But these are merely first impressions and I expect I shall modify them.
    DISTRACTIONS. I'm busy from eight o'clock in the morning until six in the evening, with an hour in between for lunch. Tea at six o'clock, the lesson at seven, by eight I've nothing to do but to go to bed or take a walk until half-past ten. For the last two evenings I've gone out with a Mr Curtis, a young, witty, clean-shaven, pipe-smoking Englishman. The evening before last, as far as Richmond. I'd tell you about it but I've no more room because I want to write you a paragraph about the way I propose to spend Saturday afternoons — my only free time except for Sunday when everything is closed, even the cafés, and asleep as if folded in prayer; a paragraph on the difficulties of understanding the different pronunciations of English; a paragraph on possible lines of study during my leisure hours: while I am here I'm going to buy a Cicero Oration annotated in English, one I have to commit to memory for the Latin exam — and I have my History. It's all I need. I hope to buy several English bedside books, in particular a book on etiquette;
    — a paragraph on food,
    — a paragraph on Francis Jammes,
    — a paragraph on the exquisite song which I enclose,
    — a paragraph on my latest purchases. It's the only one I've time to expand on at the moment. You must not enter the said purchases on the English account; I had a heap of things to buy and still have, for next term. As immediately indispensable, I've bought:

A straw hat	— 3 shillings and sixpence.
2 pairs of socks which in England are worn up to below the knee	— 2 shillings.
A tie	— 1 shilling.
3 collars	— 3 shillings.
Note-paper	— 1 shilling.

All this merely for your information since I've had lots of expenses on cabs, luggage, letters especially, which I can't hope to keep an account of.

I've sent cards off to Gagnières — Monsieur Gauthier, Marie-Rose, etc.,[3] it's expensive because of the penny stamps on the letters. Ruinous in fact.

I've still to buy a nightshirt and have the two pair of shoes I brought, resoled, etc.

Has my trunk arrived? — Was it locked — if so, have it forced open and replace the padlock which won't be of any more use.

I've just got time to write you the paragraph on food.

It's unbelievable. You're continually under the impression that you're dining with grown-up children whom you've allowed to do the dinner of their choice for a day and who have more or less transformed dinners into doll's dinner-parties.

To start with, a whole series of little knives, side-plates, little forks, little cups. *No bread!* All you have in a small plate on your left is a slice of a kind of tasteless brioche with a little butter on it that you have the right to *nibble at*. From the potato dish you are served one potato and, of course (!!) you don't even eat the bread. If only there was one single shop in London where they sold real bread!!! *No wine. Sirop* in large glasses or beer!

In the morning at half-past seven, an egg or some fish with a cup of tea with milk, bread and butter and 'marmalade' corresponding to our *confiture*.

At half-past twelve, a main dish, usually there's no bread provided, and then gooseberry tarts, jams, fish, a kind of white jelly with *marmalade*.

You eat the gooseberry tarts with a small spoon in your right hand and a small fork in your left!

At six, *we have tea* — to use the accepted expression: sardines, cake and *marmalade*, all eaten on tiny plates, and always tea with milk. All this at six o'clock, so that by eight I am, literally, starving.

I am permanently in the state I described to you when I was feverish. This time, however, I dream of robbing a bakery! Despite all these little implements on your right or left, you eat salad — without oil or vinegar — with your fingers! Salad that smells like pea-pods and which you salt yourself. It would all be enormously amusing if you were here to share the experience!

A final word to commend Guinle's Song which has matched to perfection every aim of the frivolous, desperate little poem without robbing it of its childish, nursery-rhyme nature. Try and sing it with as much light and shade as he does. A final word to tell you that I had a vague hope of managing up to the end without having to ask you for money, but because of the shoes, etc, I think it will be absolutely impossible. We'll see.

A letter will follow shortly.

Henri

Post-office, like everything else, closed on Sunday. *Not a single delivery.*

1   Where Auguste Fournier was born, in the Sologne; a place Fournier adored. See 'A travers les étés, pp. 178–82.
2   The Martin sisters, in later letters referred to as 'the two old ladies', were both teachers of French and like the Nightingales seem to have come from Lancashire.
3   Gagnières, son of the Mayor of La Chapelle; M. and Mme Gauthier, family friends; Marie-Rose, Fournier's cousin (the Marie-Louise of *Le Grand Meaulnes*).

6   TO JACQUES RIVIÈRE

For reading when you've nothing better to do.

9 July 1905   *London*

Dear old chap,
    Sunday morning, ten o'clock. Small, light bedroom on the second floor of a house hidden in greenery — on my right, through the window, a whole, distant horizon of trees and houses, all the warmth of July and the calm, immense calm of Sunday mornings in London greets me.
    On the walls: above a vaporizer, next to the gas-lamp, small texts, as in *Oiseaux de passage*, with biblical quotations which I translate for your benefit: *The Lord is thy Refuge — God first: may He prevail in all things*, etc.
    I can vaguely hear them watering the lawn below — vaguely *Mistress* (pronounced Missis) Nightingale who, like all English women, spends her time at the piano — and then, at intervals,

the whistle of a train on its way to Richmond.

Now let's pass on to details. (I'll probably confine myself to generalizations, reserving a whole host of things to tell you about in detail later.)

1. JOURNEY. PARIS-DIEPPE. I'm beginning to want to see England through the eyes of Dickens. I build up a whole little story based on an English farming couple who are sitting opposite me. I feel as if I'm starting off to spend my holidays in the English countryside as a *school-boy* from some provincial town. Of course I realize that all this is too exclusively literary!

DIEPPE. *Trans-shipment.* My impressions are becoming clearer and broadening out. It is midnight.

EMIGRANTS' DECK. Light-hearted poverty, grotesque poverty with grimy, clean-shaven faces, poverty that doesn't give a damn, poverty clasped in each other's arms . . . It is an English boat.

Sinister shouts for departure that I can't understand as we move off. We begin to walk the decks, and we're off. Out of the harbour, darkness over the sea which is about to merge into the mist beneath the brightness of a few stars; a ship like ours sails past, that is, in the mist — a space pricked out in lights. Irresistibly I think of Whistler and his Nocturnes . . . The crossing takes six hours — one hour sitting down dozing, a half-hour's stroll on deck, successively.

The sea changes its aspect from one hour to the next — milky at daybreak, with a destroyer passing far off in the morning haze.

I feel chilly even in my overcoat. I feel sorry not to be a midshipman on this ship, and wearing a navy-blue uniform, living a tough, disciplined life at sea so that some day I can go to Toulon and ask for the hand of a haughty blonde whose father has sailed the Seven Seas . . .[1]

A very young couple — they're probably eloping — fold and unfold their arms round each other, half-asleep. The girl is seasick and doesn't seem to know where to put herself. She wanders about the deck with her head lowered. The young man is excessively anxious and, with his head lowered too, asks her how she feels every two or three minutes. If I had someone to share this with, the two of us would be highly amused, even though it's all slightly depressing.

34

NEWHAVEN. First, in the distance, the white chalk cliffs (Albion), first contact with England. I don't fare too badly with my initial attempts 'in English'. From Newhaven to London, thoroughly awake, I feel a delightful thrill at the sight of this, *green*, fresh countryside — fields, huge trees, *green* meadows!

LONDON. Still this same impression of freshness. To start with, literally — since the train is perched up high — a *sea* of roofs, *immense* bridges over the Thames, trees everywhere and *immense*, clean, fragrant parks . . .

2. MY OCCUPATIONS AND MY HOSTS. Get up at seven o'clock. From eight to half-past twelve — up till now — sort the English correspondence, and am occasionally handed a letter, maybe several, to translate from English into French or conversely. Similar work from half-past one till six. Beginning this week, instead of being paid 8 shillings as agreed, I have been paid 10 shillings (10 × 1.25 frs).

Furthermore, on Monday morning, an hour after my arrival, I was introduced to the secretary of Sandersons who, next to Mr Harold Sanderson, who is never here, is the boss. He immediately had me piloted through the Chiswick area during the morning and, at half-past twelve, took me to his home to give me lunch. In the afternoon, a walk with his wife and another lady to Kew Gardens. Finally, he offered me full board and lodging at his home (a charming house like all those I've seen so far in London) at a derisory figure on condition that I give him a French lesson every day from seven to eight in the evening, as I am in fact doing; he is fair-haired and athletic, smokes a pipe in a rocking-chair, *on his lawn*, a book in his hand — with me next to him in another rocking-chair.

From eight to eleven in the evening for the last three days I've been taking a long walk with a young Englishman of about twenty-two or twenty-three, terribly witty, well read — an employee at Sanderson's, clean-shaven, pipe-smoking, who puts me wise about everything that goes on.

3. ENGLISH HOUSES. London is immense. There are countless houses like this one, and *in London* itself. I would have loved during these first few days here — neglecting trees and lawns for the time being — to have stopped and admired them one by one, at leisure. Each one is like a miniature castle — and

so different from the villas of the Paris suburbs! — with a solid, well-polished front door, windows of exquisitely coloured glass, different coloured stones, lace curtains absolutely everywhere; pianos and flutes sounding on every side.

4. MY GENERAL IMPRESSIONS OF ENGLAND.

a) *General (in the strict sense of the word)*. Initially it has been an impression of something never seen, never experienced before, of a completely new start. So much so, that on Monday afternoon, the day of my arrival, after a lunch set out like a doll's tea-party, in the manner of all English meals, when Miss Nightingale (aged eleven), fair-haired, snub-nosed, in a light coloured dress, left for Gunnersbury School, I had the feeling, bathed in the sunshine of this unknown garden where I was sitting, that I too was about to go down the warm, deserted street to attend the primary school.

b) *On the English*. Love of nature which I found delightful at first, then rather irritating. Being a practical people, they exploit it to the full. The whole of London is full of parks free of litter and empty bottles, lawns on which you may sit but not sprawl. Yet, although the effect is not artificial, it is slightly commonplace and commercial, in fact too cosy for words.

Love of flowers. Marvellous greenhouses in the parks. When the Englishman catches the scent of lime-trees, he stops short and takes in long ecstatic breaths . . . 'Oh! lovely!' I say 'the Englishman' because I have seen the most 'matter-of-fact' specimens doing it.

c) *Women*. I don't think I'll get used to it. It is like this — they are readily available but the fact is scarcely noticed. It's the normal thing to have *your girl* you walk out with, and my young English acquaintance asked me on my very first evening whether I had 'my special girl' in Paris. I was flabbergasted! And then their dresses — too homely, too short, too ordinary. For some time I've been wondering what put me off most: it was that they didn't wear corsets, so that everything they put on looks too free and easy. Add to that their bicycles, their masculine appearance and their noses in the air.

Next, houses I have long dreamed of, nature, pianos, young ladies ready at hand the whole time. I fear the result will be to cease to interest or at any rate impress me any longer. Soon, through hearing it so often, I shall no longer be afraid of no longer responding to *la séculaire tristesse qui tient dans un tout petit accord au piano.*[2]

As for English women, I have no fears from that quarter. They are so far removed from their French counterparts, who are mysterious beneath their veils, silent, remote in their salons and so feminine in their dark dresses.

5. HOW I AM GETTING ON WITH MY ENGLISH. The first days, admirably. Not so well now because I'm having doubts about it. They shower me with compliments but I still don't understand more than a quarter of the conversation going on around me, and half of what is addressed to me.

All day long at the factory I knock off commercial English at break-neck speed. You will understand that, to start with, in the middle of all the amazingly efficient administrative machinery of this factory, I felt somewhat flustered when, without a clue as to who had brought it, I was suddenly presented with a letter — or several — with these simple words, in English of course, pinned on: 'M Henri Fournier. Kindly translate and return as soon as possible. J.N.' Those first few days I didn't have a dictionary, and it was all technical jargon and commercial expressions that I'd never come across before, either in French or English. It needed a bold stroke and I managed it. My solution was to inquire of one of the young ladies who are all around me. They smile as if there was nothing to it (I mean as if they weren't young ladies) as I pressed urgently for information or rather their comments.

I am now speaking nothing but English. I've not yet reached the stage of thinking in English — that will come — but that when, for example, you translate your thoughts automatically and without hesitation — taking the precaution, as far as possible to limit them to simple things — frankly an awful business!

At frequent intervals I have fits of inward laughter (over this or that bit of nonsense); if you were here we'd split our sides.

Yesterday, overcome by one of these sudden fits that I had no one to share with, I realized how terribly lonely I was.

But these impressions, the first of which dates back a week, fade and take new shapes — now that of novelty.

One thing I can verify perfectly is the impression of time relative to the manufacture of new polygons. If you knew how

far away you, the lycée and the first Yvonne now seem.[3] I was
certainly two years old at the time. And yet, I wonder, like
Monsieur Mélinand, whether I was not then as relatively
mature as I am now and whether my dreams of those days were
not as valid as my rational thoughts of today.[4]

6. DIET.

a) If I came across a shop where they sell French bread, I
wonder what would happen. At every meal here we eat a slice
of bread and butter, a kind of tasteless brioche.

Ditto for wine. We drink *sirop* or beer in large glasses. The
last meal, tea, *at six o'clock*: so between 9 and 10 I'm starving.

b) I shan't go back to the Hanover Museum; it's really too
stupid.

7. LITERATURE. I've bought an English edition of Thomas de
Quincey's *Confessions of an English Opium Eater*. New and at
a bargain price.

In Paris I bought the July issue of the *Mercure*.[5] So don't
send it — send me *L'Ermitage* when you can and other issues of
the *Mercure*. If you like, I'll send you an 'I.O.U.' as they say in
the trade, before your holidays — or I'll pay when the new
term starts.

Very distressing, Le Cardonnel.[6] I was familiar with

> . . . *ce cri d'une girouette*
> *Ou d'une enseigne au bout d'une tringle de fer*
> *Que balance le vent pendant les nuits d'hiver.*[7]

How marvellous all the same, especially in the context of
Athalie's dream.[8] *Le Roman comique*, good.[9] I got through all
this yesterday afternoon. I've not a moment to myself the rest
of the week. I'm going to devote the whole of today to shorter
letters.

I've still a great deal to tell you. I would like to have regaled
you with an account of an unforgettable evening walk to
Richmond. To talk to you about poems I shall probably be
unable to write, especially if I am discouraged by a rejection
from *L'Ermitage*, talk to you about HER whose face suddenly
(after a period of serene near-forgetfulness, I felt her ready to
rise up like a new presence among my memories) reappeared
the other evening with such an awesome clarity that it stirred
me to the depths of my being, even to the point of tears.[10] I'm

convinced that it is something more than a little romantic adventure . . . Next time, I shall reproach you also for your whole term's silence. You could make the same effort as me surely, and try to say something to someone who will make an effort to supply everything that is left out and understand what could only be inadequately expressed in words. When you are able to write, follow my example, drop false modesty and fill the whole of ten pages just about yourself. I often think of you. Though far away from you, I am affected by your influence, your beneficient influence on me.

I often think about you.

Henri

After reading just one piece, entitled *Cette personne*, Mother has indeed written to me concerning Francis Jammes — surprisingly appropriate reflections, as if she had read all his work: '. . . it is delightful in its simplicity and truth . . . one accepts it as one accepts the sun, the storm, truth itself.' Note that my mother, unlike her son, never indulges in 'literature' in her letters and that she says all this following her remarks about what shirts I am to take.

I've commissioned Chesneau to return my correspondence — a packet of my letters, probably to Yvonne. It hadn't occurred to me to tell you, and I would have upset Chesneau if I had got him to undertake this job for you.

I am eagerly but confidently awaiting news of your exam. Practice waffling. Best of luck!

Henri

Let Guéniffey, Guinle and perhaps — to some extent — Chesneau read what seems reasonable to you for them to see. I imagine that three-quarters of my letter have no interest for you. There it is.

1   Fournier had often expressed the wish to be a sailor, and indeed spent sixteen months at the Lycée at Brest to prepare for admission to the *Borda* (naval college), but gave up the idea of a naval career. The reference to a 'haughty blonde': Yvonne de Quiévrecourt's father was a naval officer.
2   'the age-old sadness held in a simple chord on the piano'.
3   The first Yvonne, a reference to whom occurs in later letters, was Fournier's calf-love, 'her surname has never been divulged' — Robert Gibson, *The Land without a Name*, p.58.

4   Camille Mélinand, philosophy teacher at Lakanal and author of a study on childhood psychology. He later urged Fournier to read Thomas Hardy's novels.

5   *Mercure de France*: a literary review founded in 1889 by writers of the Symbolist movement.

6   Louis Le Cardonnel (1862–1936), poet and Catholic priest.

7   'ce cri d'une girouette . . .': 'this creaking of a weather-cock / or of an inn-sign on the end of an iron tringle / blowing to and fro in the wind on winter nights.'

8   A reference to the tragedy *Athalie* (1691) by Jean Racine.

9   *Le Roman comique*: satirical novel by Paul Scarron (1610–1660).

10   A reference to Yvonne de Quiévrecourt, his 'grande passion' from the time he first encountered her — 1 June 1905 — on the steps of the Grand Palais. Fournier is already obsessed with her as an unattainable ideal and a theme for literary treatment; see also his letters to Rivière when they discuss his poem 'A travers les étés'.

7   TO ISABELLE FOURNIER

[postmarked] 13 July 1905

My dear,
  Will you kindly send at the same time as the dictionary the rolls you have offered me. Only two or three as I am afraid they will be too dirty.
  Send so that my hosts cannot be displeased by seeing the contents. I kiss and thank you very much.

Henry

I was very astonished by hearing of 14 July. I had quite forgotten. Good 14 July!
  My next letter will be very unkind for you about music — regarding poetry you are lazy but not re music!
  Kisses.

Written in English, on a postcard of Turnham Green Church, marked 'during a cricket party (before the factory)'.

My Dear, Will you kindly send at the same time as the dictionary the roses you have offered to me. Only two or three, as I am afraid they will be too dirty — send so that they cannot be disfigured by seeing the contents — I Kits and thank you very much — Henry

1) I was very astonished by hearing of 14 July forgotten — good 14 July!

2) My next letter will be very wicked = regarding poesy you notre. music!

Kisses.

— I had quite forgotten for you about are tasty, but

16 July 1905

My dears,

After a fairly busy morning translating letters, with no end of journeys up and down stairs and a tiring French lesson given to Mr Nightingale, I paid a dutiful visit yesterday afternoon to the National Gallery (paintings) and the National Portrait Gallery. I came back, utterly worn out; and, in the evening, having had to put up with a visitor in the drawing-room, all I could manage was to collapse on to my bed and sleep until eight o'clock with the wonderful assurance of a full day off to come.

(This custom of giving everybody short holidays each week is very pleasant, don't you agree? They've even explained to me that it was a very practical system both for management and staff.)

This morning after taking my cold bath and getting dressed, half-an-hour's read of *Mr Pickwick* — a train journey to Richmond with Mr Nightingale during which, once again, I was thrilled to see the country, fresh and green, so close to London, lunch, tiring French lesson, I can lose myself up to six-o'clock tea-time working at my Dickens. And now, here I am writing to you late, trusting I shan't fill more than four pages, but hoping, if you behave, to send you a few brief lines, later in the week.

Although it is nearly ten o'clock, I'll take your letter to the pillar-box to stretch my legs.

It is only since my arrival here that I have suddenly felt the irresistible, physical urge to get out and 'take the air'. I also have a desire, perhaps a crazy need, to go out into the country; in my praises of London, I only seem to talk about the 'country'. During the early days especially, I always felt as if I was setting off on a holiday into the English countryside. I am quite flabbergasted to see the young factory workers go off, one by one, for a ten-day or fortnight's holiday. Just think, it's exactly nineteen years since I spent August and September in my grandmother's house — between heaven and earth (I mean with neither smoke, fog nor factory chimneys in sight).

During my walk in Trafalgar Square, Shaftesbury Rd [Avenue?] etc yesterday, I went into an English confectioners and bought a 'milk cake' and a French roll as well, so as to avoid seeming to be a tourist — which reminded me faintly of the bread of Epineuil or La Chapelle.[1] I wolfed it all in front of the startled English passers-by who are so careful to shut themselves up indoors when they eat.

I'll tell you about the English museums when I've seen a few more; so far, a slight disappointment.

I still feel the same enthusiasm for London houses. But I find the traditional distinctions between the English and French increasingly unreal and stupid. After the first few days when you say to yourself as each person comes in, speaks or passes by: 'Ah! an Englishman, an Englishwoman, I'm next to an Englishman', you soon reach the point of considering them as an abstraction composed of these peculiar little ways they express themselves, and you become aware that there are the same differences between each individual in society, the same faults, the same fussiness among the ladies . . . etc. So long as you think to yourself: these are *ladies*, they're called *Missize*, *bébés* are *babies*, it all seems different. Later, it is no longer the case. It came as no surprise.

I take a cold bath every day. It's very pleasant, but I wonder if it's a healthy practice — mama's advice, *please*?

As a slight remedy for the disadvantages of their diet, I drink water instead of lemonade or sirop. To get a pair of shoes repaired has already cost me 3 shillings and 9 pence. The other pair is being done.

Because I told you that I went out with Mr Nightingale this morning, don't get the idea that I'm getting in their way. Whether I want it or not, my life has been arranged to be quite quite independent of theirs. At first I was always afraid of having misunderstood their intentions and tended to err in the direction of excessive tact, you understand.

So far I can't place them in the equivalent French social scale. The wife, well-educated, if you like — half mama; husband — half Monsieur Bernard: financially or rather life-style, M. Bernard. But I may change my opinion.

My work: over and above the *post-book* routine, they now send up, apart from letters to translate — the odd letter with merely a note pinned on 'Please reply to this effect'. On more than one occasion already, I've had that inner and thrilling satisfaction, enjoyed by the young beginnner who is forgiven for making mistakes but has had the occasion to observe respectfully to those who advise or wish to 'correct' him that they've made a hash of it. I must be brief; it's getting late. I've left out heaps of things. I still earn my ten shillings. My laundry is extra. It's not a fiction about 'laundry in London'; I get back my collars, smooth and marvellously white. I am anxious to let you know that, since my arrival here, although I've never been so lonely and have a boring job that pins me down in an odd quarter of London and am far removed from everything I like and everything that interests me, I haven't felt depressed on a single occasion. If I were to be, it would be terrible. But up till now it's almost inexplicable. Perhaps it's due to my feeling more or less able to cope with things: language and work. I can't say. All the same, I eagerly await your letters at eight o'clock in the morning, and at half-past nine in the evening.

Kisses all round,

Henri

Yesterday I was complimented by the foreman to whom I've spoken about a dozen words in the last fortnight, *always the same trade jargon*, without his realizing that I was French or not English. It doesn't prove anything, but it's amusing.

Can I write to Isabelle for next Sunday, care of Mme Brusseau?[2]

This letter must seem futile and uninteresting. I feel embarrassed and hardly dare post it. Still, here it is!

1 Epineuil-le-Fleuriel, the small village where M. Fournier was schoolmaster from 1891 (Saint-Agathe in *Le Grand Meaulnes*); La Chapelle-d'Angillon (La Ferté-d'Angillon in the novel), where Mme Fournier's parents lived.
2 Pupils at her Lycée de Jeunes Filles (Moulin) were forbidden to receive letters from boys, even their brothers.

9 TO MARIE AND AUGUSTE FOURNIER

18 July 1905

The bread-rolls which smelt of dictionary, and were not properly baked, and were no longer fresh, were delicious.

H. Fournier

Les petits pains qui sentaient le
dictionnaire, qui n'étaient pas cuits,
et qui n'étaient plus frais
c'étaient délicieux.
H. Fournier

Grove Park, Chiswick.

7071 The "Wyndham" Series.

20 July 1905   *London*

My Friends,
  Delighted to have news of you at last. But I'd rather it hadn't cost me sixpence![1] My congratulations to Guinle, Rivière and even Guéniffey.
  I'm also wondering what can have happened to that poor imbecile, Leca. Perhaps it's because he was stupid enough to sign his masterpiece?
  Try and keep me up to date about the oral. Get Guinle to concoct a postcard for me now and then. But, I implore you, nothing on the back! It has now cost me two shillings[2] in postage-due in two days on four postcards.
  Send me the final result as soon as possible. I'll write to Rivière in a few days.
  Best wishes, and renewed congrats.

                                                    H. Fournier

P.S. In case Chesneau has gone, will one of you undertake to send on to me whatever arrives addressed to me at the Lycée? I'll settle up later. I can't send stamps and postal-orders pose a problem.

1   According to postal regulations — 'this space may be used for INLAND not Foreign Postage' — messages had to be written over the picture side itself.
2   'Six sous' in the original: sous were twenty to the franc, and the exchange rate at this time was 25F = £1 stg.

11   TO AUGUSTE FOURNIER

I'm just receiving your letter. Thank you.

20 July 1905

  It is curious enough that I have, this afternoon, *only* forgotten the first reason because I was afraid (not sure, but only afraid) to be short of money: The great feast of the factory is on Saturday evening and night. It consists in an enormous flower-show, garden-party and ball — and I am afraid — but only afraid — to have some expenses to do. So, please, let me have the order before Saturday night, if possible. Thank you, very very much — and kiss you in the same way.

I went last evening and night, by chance and only by chance, with Mr and Mrs Nightingale to the place of my last post-card 'Grove Park' that I did not know when sending and in some avenues around. It is, in my life, a deligh(t)ful — 'unforget(t)able' walk.

I kiss you.

Henri

I'm just receiving your letter. Thank you.

Written in English, on a postcard of the Houses of Parliament and Westminster Hall.

47

23 July 1905   *London*

My dear Jacques,

I think that by the time this reaches you, everything will be more or less over — and I pray the good Lord that it will have ended satisfactorily. The news of your admissibility has, as you thought, been no surprise to me; the news of the others has greatly encouraged me for next year — although I realize that later on there'll be the oral, the whole of that terrible oral which is now putting you on the rack.

Ergo, I am, believe me, eagerly and *impatiently* waiting to hear the result.

Now, as I've no idea about what your present interests are, I'm going to chat for these few pages about mine and I hope that you, in your turn, will be interested.

Well, outwardly, I'm leading the most negative life you can imagine. Departure for the factory at half-past eight. Return home, six o'clock. Otherwise, little or nothing. However, these last three days, my life, I fear, seems about to broaden out. But let's start by putting things in order:

THE FEMININE SEX. It is here, I think, where there is the greatest difference between the English and the French, and, once again, I have to take into account that in France I have never mixed with the kind of girls I meet here.

First let me tell you of a little adventure with a little English girl. It's gently amusing — not more — and then, in the course of the story, I'll give you a vague idea of my life:

In the office where at the present moment I'm working *ten* minutes every hour and where, the rest of the time, I am doing English grammar — and even more agreeable work, as I shall explain in a later chapter — I have in front of me, on the far side of a huge desk piled up with dictionaries, thick ledgers, typewriters, three young ladies. Behind me, separated from me by a glazed partition, a whole team of cashiers bent over their accounts and, finally, in various parts of the office, in telephone booths, other young ladies . . .

Two of the three are very handsome, amazing. They spend their time creating opportunities to flirt with the first employee on the scene. Very nice girls they are, but as their mode of behaviour puts me off, and as I prefer not to have anything in common with them or their cashiers, I confront their perpetual giggling with a *chilly silence* or the 'absent-minded' air of a man who has something better to think of.

The third is the one to whom I was first introduced and was to explain things to me. (I only know her surname and as it resembles a certain French first-name, I feel unable to tell you it out of consideration for you.)

I had immediately registered a fine pair of eyes, a body you're not aware of; she looks twenty-three but must be nineteen. Funny little head. Perfect nose, prominent chin, but very nice all the same.

And then the rest of the time, while filing my letters or looking up words, I realized that she was shy and reserved. And then on two or three occasions, despite the 'no talking' rule, she had managed to make some pleasant remarks:

'Mr So and So who has just come into the office is back from his holidays. I shan't be instructing you any longer ...'
'Weren't you surprised to see that...' And then, I normally so reserved with everybody, one fine evening at six o'clock when she was picking up, or attempting to pick up her huge ledgers in her tiny arms to put them away, rush forward — in a flash they've disappeared into the safe — and off I go with, a 'Thank-you' (*merci*) from her, a smile and a blush...

Two days ago, Miss Nightingale took pots of various flowers to her school. There was to be a flower-show and competition of the kind now taking place throughout London, for schools, factories and clubs. As is customary on this occasion, a garden-party takes up the whole afternoon and the little girls sold ice-cream up to eleven o'clock (respectable hour; after that, everything closes down). Miss Nightingale had invited me to come and buy ices from her. For a joke I asked her the price — pretty dear! For a joke Mr Nightingale, in a tone which I could have supposed was to spare me any embarrassment, had said: 'You've somewhere to go this evening I think, young lady?' Finally, after tea, about seven o'clock, I had almost forgotten Miss Nightingale and I didn't go along. I left the house to post a letter. I knew that the school was 'affiliated' to a church and it seems that the exhibition and all that followed, might well have taken place in the building. In any case, I didn't even know where it was . . .

. . . On the way to the post which is quite a distance, I notice the illuminated entrance to a churchyard. There's a programme on the door. I don't miss the opportunity of reading and noting the words. I come to the last item: 'walk *ad libitum* in the illuminated garden until 11 pm', when Mr and Mrs Nightingale pass close to me. The husband stays chatting with me. I'm just moving off to the post when Mrs Nightingale begs us to go in to see her daughter's prize . . .

I go in. At first all I see in a little garden are clumps of bushes decorated with 'fairy-lights', as the English call them. Then a profusion of bunches of flowers or plants right along the wall of the strange little church with its faintly glowing stained-glass windows. Next, groups of youths with the handsome girls from the office. Finally a group of nice girls, one of whom, oddly dressed with a strange little Directory hat,[1] moves away from the others, greets the Nightingale family and comes towards me with her hand held out: my little English girl! And there we both stay. I make fantastic efforts to understand everything and *do* understand it all. It is obvious that she's made a great effort to come and talk to me. The English words I hear her say are fixed in my memory along with the little private life peculiar to them this evening . . . I hear her use 'should' for 'would' in the second person plural to express obligation, 'ought' instead of the simple conditional and I'll always remember it: 'You *should have* (you ought to have) come sooner . . .' The words she prompts me with when I hesitate, like 'fairy-light', I'll remember too. And then we say sweet nothings which could only be said from beneath a little Directory hat or by someone who has an imperfect knowledge of English: 'I go to church every Sunday, that's why I'm here . . . I'm going on holiday tomorrow. Ten days is a very short time. — Oh! I'm going to feel awkward now. — Oh no, the work isn't difficult for you, is it?' Like all English women she is enormously addicted to this discreet way of saying 'n'est-ce pas?', which consists in repeating the verb employed in an interrogative way, using only the auxiliary verb and the subject (with a negative if the proposition was affirmative, without negation if it was negative). 'Oh, you can't understand them because they have a suburban accent? And I've got it too, haven't I? ... It's very pretty, the church wall hidden by the foliage, the flowers and the coloured glass, isn't it?' It is this 'isn't it' which recurs so often ... I stay on nearly an hour with a special kind of pleasure which, because of the church and the hat, I describe to myself as 'methodist'. Then I take leave of her, shaking her hand and saying, although it is usually just addressed to men, but because I really think it:

'I am very pleased to have seen you.'

And then I go back through the streets alone, alone but not depressed (not once for a month now) thinking:

'Yes, but *le bateau faisait un bruit calme* . . .'[2] And I think only of the Seine, the avenue and Toulon.

FEMININE SEX (Second part). Yesterday, Saturday afternoon, an enormous exhibition of flowers and garden-party from half-past two until eleven o'clock in the evening at the club and in the factory gardens. Every year for the last four years they've been trying (and now and then during the year) to get the 'gentlemen' and the workers to mix, but they hardly mix at all. I'm introduced to a Spaniard who speaks perfect French and English and who is now going to hook on to me all the time. All through the afternoon I can't take a step in the garden without a smart and courteous foreman introducing me and putting two or three young English girls in my charge for half-an-hour or an hour. It's a bore but I carry it off very well.

From time to time I catch sight of a young lady's dress of exquisite lightness passing in the distance; its owner has lips and eyes which remind me of the *Girl with the Lamb* by Greuze which I saw last Sunday — with a profile and grace which set me thinking for a long time in the afternoon, I can't imagine why, perhaps because of a certain photograph, about a certain person you know but I don't.

Exquisite too (alas!) the dress, the *black Directory hat* with a large ribbon that passes below the chin, and the small head with black eyes of a little girl the courteous foreman entrusted to me in the gardens *between ten and eleven*. But when, after having conveyed her wish to be allowed to accompany me this evening to some exhibition or other in London — which I am almost inclined to grant — she begins to seem somewhat over-eager to forego dancing to go off with me, to ask for cigarettes and

51

inquire how many 'hearts I've already broken in France', I am furious with the courteous foreman and take the first opportunity of palming off the young English girl who *also*, alas, uses *isn't it* and *what a shame* (you can't dance, *what a shame*!) in the most charming manner.

That was last night at eleven o'clock. It is now nine o'clock this morning. Forgive my telling you all this. It's so uninteresting for anyone who hasn't got to live another two months among these different classes of English society.

ARTS (Painting section). I've lacked the strength of mind to interest myself in the *National Portrait Gallery*. Nothing but portraits! Nothing but portraits! I looked at those of Bentham and Spencer.

The *National Gallery*, very artistic in general arrangement and very comfortable, in its range more like the Luxembourg than the Louvre.[3] The foreign and medieval schools especially are magnificently represented. I took a particular interest in items I already knew.

I saw the Rembrandt portrait — a self-portrait as an old man which, in my opinion, is almost as good as *Saint somebody or other with the Angel*.[4] The same beam of light falling on the hands, in the shadow. Lots of others by him in the same vein. *An Old Woman*, *Rabbis*, *A Burgomaster*, etc., then, very different: his bold, naturalistic, opulent and luxurious *Rape of the Sabine Women*. And a somewhat low-key, very naturalistic *Woman bathing*.[5]

Quite a number of Téniers that one feels moved to rediscover: *The Conversation*: three men meditating a 'dirty trick' as Chesneau would say, and the wife of one of them waiting inquisitively at the door or perhaps trying to overhear. *Playing at Bowls* — always the same background: small old houses of an old, tiny village in the remote countryside.

Giovanni Bellini's *The Doge*. (I'm reeling them off as they occur to me.) Pale, impassive, angular, amazing.

Ecstasy in front of the van Eyck: the husband with the large hat and his wife, pregnant I think.[6] No need to describe it, you know it. But you get a much deeper impression than from any slide of the picture.

La Fontaine by Chardin.

Charles I by Van Dyck.

A Girl with a Lamb by Greuze.

A Child with an Apple by Greuze.

And then, reminding me of the last two, in an entirely different part of the gallery:

The Shrimp Girl by Hogarth which thrilled me — only a sketch.

But my great thrill is John Constable's *The Valley Farm*, and above all, Turner.

The Valley Farm. Green and maroon, the end of a valley, a farm — perhaps, vaguely, horses and a figure. Fresh, old-world impression. You feel it should be called the *Valley-Cottage*. I'm wrong, it is all brown.

And then the staggering Turner. A gallery to himself. Staggering because, unless I'm mistaken, there are pictures dated 1830 or 40 which would seem daring even today in the National Collection of the Grand Palais.

A Train passing in the storm, rain and steam at full speed over an iron bridge.[7] Nothing but white, black and red, it is gripping in its truth.

Queen Mab's Cave. Black and red.

Petworth Park. Very English green.

Then a host of things on Venice, leaving me stunned as I sat before them on one of the seats with which each gallery is comfortably provided.

The painting called *Approach to Venice* is composed wholly in gold, warm white and red with something that looks like one or more ships of silk and gold sailing towards the setting sun and Venice.

It is at once bold and old-fashioned and so, doubly impressive; similar impression in front of his *Ulysses deriding Polyphemus*, ships, caves, rocks, dragons, sun and sea and his *Childe Harold's Pilgrimage* which reminds one of the voyage to Greece and all his other Venetian paintings.

But the unique masterpiece is the *Approach to Venice*. And the train on the bridge gives the impression of revolutionary daring (nothing old-fashioned here!).

I've not been able to dwell on a number of his other pictures, several of which are still more daring, some of a quite different kind, several excellent, quite a few not so good.

Some days after my visit to the *National Gallery*, I discovered the *Mercure* article on Turner, etc. Tristan Leclère has rightly called him the 'Poet of Venice who makes every tone sing in a silvery or golden light'.

But all that dates. At the same time I'm searching in vain for contemporary English painters as well as English primitives.

It would be very nice if you were to ask me to go and look at some particular individual painter that you know, since I go into it more or less blindfold.

Today I'm going to the British Museum if I can. And then tomorrow, Monday, until midday Saturday, I shall resume my little life of solitary thought, disturbed neither by pictures nor passers-by.

LITERATURE

1. A disappointment has been with me all week. I ordered *Mélanges posthumes* from a French bookseller.[8] All sorts of reasons persuaded me. I would so much like to know something about his private life, although perhaps I know it more profoundly through his verse, and then his notes on *l'Art en Allemagne* and on *La Femme*. I've been very disappointed because the book hasn't come in. Very. If it is out of print, I shall buy *Le Triomphe de la vie* or *Le Deuil des primevères*.[9]

To the bookseller who immediately categorized me mentally as one of those wealthy Frenchmen visiting London for a couple of months for pleasure purposes and anxious not to miss the latest titles and had got out for me the 'Bazin's', *Marie Krysinska* etc., I remarked 'What, you haven't any Laforgue or Jammes in stock — but look here, in France they are the *only* ones that count!' And I was as pleased as Punch with this small if distant blow struck for Francis Jammes and Laforgue.

The bookseller was so taken aback that he kept on calling me 'Monsieur Jules Laforgue'!

2. I'm quite prepared, as I said before, to pay whatever *L'Ermitage* and the *Mercure* cost to make sure of getting them, but not before the new term, as it is impossible to send stamps. Naturally I will even pay my five sous for the July *Mercure*. I'm not a cad [*salaud*] like Guinle.

3. After ten days of total blankness, following exacting work, and a fear of being unable to produce a single line of poetry these last three months, I had the enormous satisfaction of producing some last Sunday at this same hour, and a whole

week spent completing the second part of my piece — the calmest and most remote — between two expeditions. All this amid the factory din and *in the factory* itself! Quite a triumph, don't you think? I'm delighted and have lots of ideas.

As for my 'piece' (taking its title from the opening: 'A travers les étés . . .') I've said everything I wanted to say about HER. I've said everything I've thought concerning her and nothing more. But I have said it all, all I wanted to say.

It starts off with lots of *vers libres* which, at first sight, look like so many truncated alexandrines; but I think I've managed to prove to young Bernès that it has, nevertheless, more power than cut-up alexandrines.[10]

My sole and very real worry is that, en route I seem to have encountered Francis Jammes three or four times. I was afraid of that, and two or three times it has quite put me out. But, it can't be helped.

Consequently, I've dedicated my piece:

A une jeune fille
A une maison
A Francis Jammes

I'll remove the dedication *A Francis Jammes* if you don't think of Francis Jammes as you read it, but, on the other hand, I shan't mind leaving it in. You will realize that I'm not in a position to judge at the moment.

A thing that proves my absolute sincerity is that it is the subject itself — the house — which brings Francis Jammes most to mind — it goes back to my tender years — and above all the old lady who did exist as I said, was light-hearted as I described her and made me think of our Sunday calls on old ladies throughout my childhood.

And you'll understand without any prompting on my part how, in spite of myself, I've been able to encounter Francis Jammes without sacrificing my sincerity.

I'm going to send it to Guéniffey who will pass it on to you (you = Guinle and yourself) — this poor Guéniffey whom perhaps — put off by his smile — I've somewhat neglected lately.

The hundreds of things I've still to tell you will come along each Sunday bit by bit. I simply must talk to you about Dickens who has moved me to tears in the English text. I think I've sorted out the things I admire him for and the essence of his genius.

I shall doubtless be telling you about two old ladies, French teachers, who live close by. Here are the literary works they've confessed their admiration for so far: 'Madame what's her name' (all the English are talking about it), and . . . *Télémaque*.[11]

The great genius for the rest of the English people I know is Alexandre Dumas, père. I don't think that it will strike you as at all surprising. I'm hoping to have the opinion of my young English girl (from Cambridge)[12] on Kipling. I've heard him spoken of as a very uneven and sometimes — it's the English expression — very 'poor' author.

As I'd received no word from Yvonne,[13] I finally sent her a postcard in English addressed to her home — a couple of lines in which I gave her until today to return my most recent letters. Next Monday or Tuesday I'm going to request her father politely and briefly to be good enough to get her to return my letters in exchange for hers which she can't have any feelings about. Regarding *her* letters, I'm on strong ground, you realize. I've nothing to fear from my family to whom her father can write without doing me any harm, since my parents know the whole story more or less and, nothing could please them more than a breaking-off of relations. My only apprehension is of a scandal coming from the lycée quarter — an open letter, sent expressly . . . etc. But I don't care a rap and perhaps I can wait for the holidays with nothing else to fear. I am not giving way — or very little — to any wish for revenge. All I want is that everything should be over between us, you understand.

If there's any justice left in France, you will go up and collect my prize (2nd Prize for Gymnastics) at the Distribution. It would be very good of you.

Three days ago I went out at twilight for the third time into the suburban neighbourhood around Grove Park where the house which pleased both Milton and Cromwell still stands.[14] I felt more than admiration, it was real emotion. Always the same gentle stirrings of the heart as I pass along these quiet rows of exquisite houses with their little lights, little windows, subtle colours and lace curtains. So exquisite as to bring tears to one's eyes — houses where you imagine souls, souls . . .

Till next time then, my dear fellow. I'm longing for your first letter. You see that I tell you everything, everything you can discover about yourself as your pen runs on, nothing much, but the best I can do. You do the same.

Soon then.

Your friend,

Henri Fournier

1   Refers to the extravagant fashions created in the 'Directoire' period, 1795–1799.
2   Alain-Fournier repeats this almost in the same words in the scene in *Le Grand Meaulnes* where Meaulnes finds himself in a little boat with the châtelaine: 'Le bateau filait avec un bruit calme . . .' (I:15). The garden-party is the seed of the much romanticized 'fête étrange' in the novel.
3   The Musée du Luxembourg was installed in the Orangerie of the Palais du Luxembourg in 1886, and the collection remained there until 1939. After the war, most of the contents were dispersed among other galleries in Paris.
4   Fournier refers to Rembrandt's *The Angel Leaving Tobias and his Family*, now in the Louvre.
5   While the paintings Fournier mentions are clearly by Rembrandt, the one that is 'very different' is likely to be by Rubens, whose *Rape of the Sabines* was in the National Gallery, and being Flemish was probably in the same room.
6   Jan van Eyck: *The Arnolfini Marriage*.
7   Turner's *Rain, Steam, and Speed: the Great Western Railway*.
8   *Mélanges posthumes* (1903) by Jules Laforgue (1860–87): prose pieces, including 'Notes sur la femme' and 'L'Art en Allemagne'.
9   *Le Deuil des primevères*, 1901, elegies by Francis Jammes; *Le Triomphe de la vie*, 1902, also by Jammes.
10   Bernès was a Classics master at Lakanal. 'A travers les étés': written during the summer of 1905, the poem has elements that foreshadow *Le Grand Meaulnes*. See letter no. 40.
11   *Télémaque* (1699), written by Fénelon for the edification and amusement of the Duc de Bourgogne.
12   Fournier had been corresponding with Lilian Weber for two years, and arranged to meet her on his last day in London. See letters nos. 13, 21, 24, 39, 42.
13   The 'first' Yvonne, not Yvonne de Quiévrecourt.
14   This house was demolished in 1928, after the death of the last owner. The connection with Milton and Cromwell is obscure; perhaps Fournier is confusing it with Chiswick.

23 July 1905

My dear little sister,

I'm very distressed not to be allowed to write to you. I had heaps of things to tell you and some (especially one) to send you. It will be for the end of September. It's a long way off. Write to me often from home, I am *so lonely* here.

Either on the day of your departure or on your way through Bourges, could you oblige me greatly by sending for me one or two (pretty and original) postcards of the locality

1. to Miss Clare Nightingale — 5 Brandenburgh Rd, Gunnersbury, London W with some such message as: 'Isabelle Fournier sends her best wishes to Miss C.N.'

2. to Miss Lilian Weber — 114 Chesterfield Rd, St. Andrew's Park, Bristol with 'For Miss Lilian's album from H.F., with kindest regards from I.F.' It would be very kind of you. Thank you.

N.B. Write only on this side of the card. I am really very sorry not to be allowed to write to you.

Kisses.

Henri

25 July 1905

My dear Dears,

Let us take things in order:

First, you are frightfully lucky to be seeing little *Isabelle* the day after tomorrow, to be kissing her and spending two months with her, dear little creature, in some cosy corner of the house. Here I sometimes take an hour's stroll imagining I'm in her company and I find an interest in a heap of things that I wouldn't have noticed otherwise. When we both are teachers, we will certainly repeat the journey together.

While waiting for that distant day, I will be very pleased to look after *Monsieur and Madame Gauthier*. Ever since hearing they were able to come, that is to say the whole of last Sunday afternoon, I've been making a note of street-names and tramway stops. Let them try and come on a Saturday and they'll have me for the whole of Saturday afternoon and the whole of Sunday. On other days, I am free from 6 o'clock in the evening until midnight. (In England you go to bed between 10 and 11. At Mr Nightingale's (Naitinguèle) they drink milk with their tea. It's an excellent beverage and I commend it to you who have kilos of Royal Tea in store. But they drink one or two cups, not — as you did on one occasion — a whole bowl.) So, I'll be very pleased if Mr and Mrs G. come. They ought to start learning some English words. Tell them how nice of them (an English turn of phrase) it was to send me this vast view of the Loire, and how wistfully I contemplated it!

MY AMUSEMENTS. Saturday, from a quarter-past two onwards until eleven o'clock at night a terrific party at the factory. Exhibitions and flower-shows like those everywhere in London at the moment, accompanied by a garden-party. A garden-party? Do you remember what I used to get the village kids to do in the playground to amuse me: run races of every possible kind, sack-races, wheelbarrow races, etc, etc. Imagine that, only the village kids replaced by *ladies* and gentlemen — and the order and very simple organization of the races all worked out beforehand — and you'll have some idea of a garden-party. Add to this, in the evening, from 8 to 9, choirs and songs involving these same ladies and gentlemen, from 9 to 11, a dance. (But not later than 11 on a Saturday night because, hang it! everybody's got to be home by midnight — after midnight it's Sunday and nobody budges!)

N.B. It all takes place on a lawn no bigger than your garden. The ladies and girls run 20 yards with an egg in a spoon, or have an arithmetical sum to work out or a needle to thread. All the same, this idea of getting people to bestir themselves in such an undignified way would never occur to anyone in France. The most fascinating thing about it all is the idea they've had for some years now of trying to get the gentlemen and the workers to mix. But they hardly ever do, and one lot merely provides a source of amusement for the other — without fail.

As for myself, I wasn't able to walk a couple of yards all evening without being landed with two or three girls. I had to manage somehow, and I did. But it's so normal here to have girls with you that no one takes any notice. You don't have any of the Frenchman's pleasant embarrassment when he is entrusted with a partner.

To return to what I was telling you: the day before yesterday, there were some *ravishing* dresses at that fête: the large Directory hat tied under the chin with fluttering watered-silk ribbons, and wonderfully floating dresses. You get used to it; and then, it's still ravishing.

Sunday morning you get up late. For those who attend a *Service*, it's not until 11. When you wake up, you are impressed by the silence of the vast city. So far, Sunday mornings have been cool and cloudy. You have the sensation of infinite peace; because of all the trees and foliage you see, it is as if the vast town had got up early this Sunday in order to go out into the countryside to sleep. It would take very little to make it depressing, and that would be a pity. You hardly ever have lunch before 2 o'clock. I feel more and more famished, with Mrs Nightingale who always has a way of saying: *'Do you wish another cake more?'* emphasizing the *do you wish* as if to say *'You must not wish, you have enough!'* She and her daughter are singularly unattractive, but not to me; I try to think of something else when I see them, that's all; if, as George Sand said, you killed everything that's unattractive, you'd be committing suicide more than once in your life! All you can do is to cut them out of *your own* life; it's what I am doing when I direct my thoughts elsewhere.

I'll go on with the account of my Sunday in London. The afternoon is depressing. Shops closed. Luckily you have the museums, but not all. You go home at 6 o'clock to have your cup of tea, your bread-and-butter or, if you like, bread and jam; if you prefer not, you can take tea in a confectioner's. In either case you can imagine how empty you feel by bedtime and how you long to buy yourself some cakes.

Last Sunday I went to the South Kensington Museum [Victoria and Albert] which is surrounded with annexes. I don't know of anything vaster than this museum. There are vistas of rooms of cut glass, antique scuplture, jewellery — cold, cold, stretching to infinity. Thousands of primitive artefacts in the annexes, endless art from Japan. This Japanese art is so novel and exquisite! I'd love to talk to you about it, and about the Constable and Turner paintings which I've made into something of a speciality, but I've told Rivière all about it in my letter of a fortnight ago. It's more important to him than to you and I don't feel energetic enough to repeat all the paragraphs I've already written to him.

I expect you know that the English have a rather childish love of the original document, of the wall behind which something happened. So that along with the paintings, all the rooms of their museums contain letters from painters, their last palette, and so forth. It was a moving experience to see the manuscripts of Dickens's novels (when you see the simplicity of his style you can hardly credit all the crossings-out). The final page of a novel he penned before losing consciousness. The letter to the illustrator Maclise,[1] serious from beginning to end, and written in the way you might write about the death of a holy man, concerns the loss of his pet raven. And I saw

Maclise's letter to Mr Forster, or rather the sheet of paper which he enclosed with the letter from Dickens when he sent it to Mr Forster, and on which he had sketched the 'Apotheosis of the Raven'. The black corpse of the raven from which rises a *totally white* Apotheosis raven, soaring up to join a Trinity of ravens, feet close together in the clouds. It is all fascinating. But there's not a soul in these vast rooms where, now and then, a step, a voice echo. I expect it's crowded on a Saturday or rather, during the week.

I saw also the Millets (engravings) from Isabelle's book, along with lots of others. Of absorbing interest.

In the evening I went out just before 10 o'clock. On Sundays no one goes to bed after ten. No theatres, nothing. You're supposed to spend the whole day at church services. A surprise: at two or three street corners, hymns, a banner, a lantern, a small platform. I approach, thinking they're street-singers and amazed to find them singing in the street on a Sunday, and I read on the banner: *Chiswick Baptist Church*. After the six o'clock services and from six to ten o'clock, amid all the din of the street, the trams and passers-by, it's simply the church and the good God who trot round for the benefit of those — too poor to dress properly, or hardened sinners they have to seek out — who haven't been able to attend a service. There are four or five women, some children and three or four men who are singing hymns; passers-by, 'those who wish' (here, it's always 'those who wish') stop and join in the singing. When the hymns are over, one of the men steps forward; he looks poor and simple-minded but for three-quarters of an hour, in the middle of the street, hat on head, he delivers to the circle of bystanders or believers who stand rooted to the spot — a hell-fire sermon which I understand from the first word to the last because he shouts, proceeds slowly and mostly uses the simple, time-honoured language of the Bible — a sermon in which this leitmotiv recurs: '*How shall we escape!*' he shouts, '*How shall we escape if we neglect the great Salvation! How shall we escape*'.[2] And he compares *us* in succession to men asleep in a house on fire, or in a ship in peril on the sea, etc . . . all this howled with the greatest vehemence. How shall we be saved!! And the passers-by who don't wish to stop, pass by as if nothing was happening. I am looking forward to the pleasure of showing all this to Monsieur Gauthier without warning him beforehand. When I come back, I'll give you my imitation of a lay preacher. It will amuse you. All evening it's been running through my head: How shall we be saved!!

In the street they suddenly hand you out an edifying yet terrible pamphlet, if you want it, full of devils and illustrations of sins.

What's more, on the Metropolitan line, high up between advertisements for matches or rice powder, I was amazed to discover in each carriage, a frame reserved for verses from the Bible or from the Gospels. 'The Sinner, the Evil one, Infinite Mercy, etc . . .' which you can read *if you wish*.

A final word, for I'm tired of writing. You can't imagine the vastness of London. I've not been able to realize it myself yet. The outer railings of Hyde Park run for miles. And London is divided into districts, subdivided into E, W, SE, SW, etc. You can't hope to go on foot from any one place to another as in Paris. You'd soon find yourself lost.

I am persuaded that, more than the Tommy Atkins who write two or three lines to their parents to ask for a birth certificate, I have a right to say to you 'I have nothing else to tell you for the present'.

Ask Isabelle to write me nice long letters. They're my only pleasure here. I must talk to you next about postmen and soldiers. You must ask me about anything that comes into your head. Papa is being rather unkind not to write to me now that the holidays approach.

Forgive my writing to you on these pages from my notebook, but I always carry it in my pocket — I continue the letter when I want, it's more convenient than a large sheet of paper.

Kisses all round.

Henri

Yesterday evening a letter arrived from Jean [Bernard]. It was much longer and more interesting than he usually writes and well written — easy to read in fact (not a single exclamation mark).

Tell him that I said this to you. He'll be pleased and it will make him repeat the effort.

No news from Paris, but I realize that there's some difficulty but also some real hope — no comment — just wait.

Of course, I've never said anything about your political and literary plans.

Henri

It would be sensible of you to pay some attention to those cheap newspaper articles, although at the worst they can only frighten primary school inspectors who have no idea of the sources. I wonder in what way it can harm you since it's politics that rules everything and that père Jublot is not politics.[3] He can't obtain a tobaconnist's shop for his son, he won't make you change. After all, what can it do to you?

Only, be sensible, I mean, stick together, be as straightforward as possible and only get angry if pushed to the limit. This is what you've done so far, and done well.

Kisses.

Henri

Monday, 4.45 pm

I too was upset, I assure you, to find myself obliged to ask you for money so soon.

I thought I could still rub along for a long time with what I had left, once the main expenses were accounted for.

I am distressed to hear that you are upset about it. But, I assure you, I'm living a very impoverished, Dickensian petty clerk kind of life, leaving for the office at eight, returning at six for tea, paying out for the occasional tram ride on Sunday or in the evening, etc, or for museums on Sunday.

Let's take the journey, for example.

You mention 35 francs, but you should also take into account the cab which transported my suitcase to the Gare St Lazare and the fact that I was in a hurry and had to pay in consequence because Monsieur Bernard was waiting for me at midday to sign your registered letter the postman was to bring me. You should add the tip for the carrying of the suitcase which I had to put in the left-luggage office because of its weight, and for the transport 3 francs or more. Also the cab when I arrived in London (*le handsome*) which took me to Berners Street for an exorbitant charge.

Just one of the hundreds of things you don't anticipate as arrival expenses: the exchange rate.

But that's all over now; there'll only be the regular expenses.

I'm sorry to tell you that this evening for the first time I'm being involved in extra expense at this very moment — for I write to you from the factory — in short, two young fellows recommended to me by Mr Nightingale, one English, the other Spanish, whom I met on Saturday afternoon and both of whom seem to me in fact very recommendable, have just proposed to take me to the Lyric Theatre [Hammersmith] this evening — very good, comfortable seats at sixpence each (12 sous!).

They are playing an English-type melodrama — very black and against the Russians. *Under the Tsar* is its title.

You will shortly be having a long and interesting letter from me.

Kisses (keep some for Isabelle).

Henri

Forgive the notebook page written in the factory din.

1 Daniel Maclise (1806–70), close friend of Dickens and John Foster (Dickens's biographer), a caricaturist and portrait painter.
2 Fournier would have noticed later the use of such a text, painted on a stile, in his reading of *Tess of the D'Urbervilles* (chapter XII).
3 Père Jublot was a Justice of the Peace at La Chapelle. Tobacco is a state monopoly in France, and therefore the tenancy of tobacconists can depend on political string-pulling.

15 TO MARIE AND AUGUSTE FOURNIER

30 July 1905

My Dears,

Last night, thanks to papa's letter, some of the happiness from Isabelle's arrival, the first conversations, the excitement of unpacking . . . spilled over on to me. Yesterday evening, thanks to papa, I was able to share a fragment of your life of Friday. That was yesterday evening at half-past nine, the evening before this gloomy, idle, lonely day; it gave me the courage to endure it. So I thank him for his excellent letter and now expect one a week from him up to the end of the present term.

I am now continuing this letter at half-past seven p.m., on my return from an outing in which Mr Nightingale suddenly invited me to take part along with a young man from the provinces passing through London. The expedition turned out to be excessively costly and it forces me to raise a question which is beginning to make me despair.

Out of the 11 shillings that I received from you on Saturday the 22nd, I've spent:

	s.	d.
Saturday, 22nd.		
my board (12 sh.) . . .	2	
my laundry . . .	1	5
a packet of cigarettes to hand round in the evening . . .		6
lemonade (the usual drink offered) . . .		6
Saturday, 29th		
my board (12 sh.) . . .	2	
my laundry . . .	1	3
During the week		
Theatre and tram . . .		8
tram and tube for the town (once on Monday, 23rd and twice during the week, in the evening; the tram costing 2d return, the tube 4d) . . .	1	6
Twice, 1 additional tea . . .		10
Correspondence, stamps (for 3 letters and 3 p.c.'s) 10½		
post-cards — 3 . . .		3
Today's expedition to Hampton Court		
Boat (outward) . . .		6
train to boat . . .		3
train (return) . . .		6
lunch . . .		6

14.8 (13/6½)

one shilling = 1.25 (1 py)
one penny = 0.10
one shilling = 2 sixpence = 12 pence.

I beg you to believe that I'm not inventing or hiding anything. I beg you to note, too, that, apart from today's expedition which I would not have treated myself to on my own, my expenses are normal. It wasn't just to see what it was like that I bought a 12 sous ticket for a Music Hall with two foreigners or because, like everyone else, I wanted to hand round cigarettes, that justifies anyone saying I am causing unnecessary 'expenses'. All I treat myself to are one or two tram rides on Sundays or in the evenings when I feel I must get out, or to a cup of tea when I'm not too desperately hungry. I'm allowing myself absolutely nothing extra. I've told you the strict truth. So you see I can't possibly manage.

1. Because of the dust and smoke in the factory, I frequently have to change my linen, hence the bill for 1/- and more each week.

2. By way of explanation for the supplementary teas, I'd like to quote you this week's *regular* menu which hasn't varied by a single cake the whole week.

Morning. White coffee, a cup (not a bowl) with bread and butter.

Midday. A cutlet with three potatoes and butter (no bread and butter), a slice of gooseberry tart, a glass of water thrown in, and I'm off.

Six o'clock. A cup of tea with milk and a slice of bread and butter, a little jam on the bread and butter.

I beg you to believe that I'm not exaggerating. Moreover, I am sure that this house is one of those where you are considered to be well fed.

The table is laid out with small plates, set on small embroidered table-mats and small forks. What makes matters worse is that when I go out in the evening, however economical I am, I can't hold out any longer, and, about nine o'clock, I buy another cup of tea (there's no help for it if you want to buy cakes to take away; otherwise they look on you as a beggar).

3. As far as today's trip is concerned, I would gladly have turned it down, but I had no choice. We set off before supper, taking the friend from the provinces along with us, and we didn't get back until six o'clock. As soon as the first train fare had to be paid, I rushed forward to pay for my seat — then it was agreed that Mr Nightingale should do the same for me as well as for the provincial friend and would make a note of the amount. I got a nasty shock, especially when I saw what the

boat fare was, but I made it plain that I did not want to rob him of a double fare. Mr Nightingale, for whom I have an increasing admiration, would have paid the whole amount without hesitation . . . but . . . there's a Mistress Nightingale!

I'm sorry to have to begin by talking (perhaps exclusively) about this little expedition on account of the expenses involved. I am referring to the Palace of Henry VIII [Hampton Court], some fifteen miles from London and surrounded by possibly the loveliest park and gardens in the world. The impressions I bring away will certainly be among the deepest in my life — as much for their novelty as for the old memories they delightfully, albeit a little wistfully, stirred up in me. But about all these feeling, talkative though I may have been, you can be sure that the Englishman and his friend from the provinces had absolutely no idea!

But to return to the tedious matter of expense: this evening I am, once again, *short of cash*. This morning I began my letter calm but contented, without of course suspecting that I was going to have to end it this evening or rather stop harping on this dismal subject. And last evening, hearing the cheerful news about Aunt Mevenne's present without any mercenary thoughts, I was far from suspecting that today I would be eager to see it arrive as soon as possible to enable me to make ends meet. 'No, no, how disgusted I am with myself!' as Chesneau used to say.

Suddenly, last week, they once more foisted on me this boring postal service they had relieved me of. I discovered that despite all his efforts, Mr Nightingale had found no alternative. 'All his efforts' — mind you — merely means that probably for a couple of seconds he tried to hold up the complex machinery of the factory at the cost of making a comment to Mr Sanderson which was found unacceptable and that everything went on as usual. So now, eight times a day, I have to carry letters. On two occasions I had to take a satchel because there was an overflow. It seemed a bit hard, and for a moment my heart sank, but I consoled myself by recalling that I had wanted to come to England at any cost and that the whole service required of me amounted to carrying on my back the parcels usually carried by the boy.

When, on the first of July, I found myself in possession of

such a large sum, I said to myself now I'd always have money in hand, and here I am back to struggling to make ends meet.

My need to get out into the country, to drink milk and eat grass for a couple of days was so urgent that I had said to myself: 'come the first, short holiday, that shall be my treat'. As well as Saturday afternoon and Sundays, we have got next Bank Holiday Monday, but all my plans have gone by the board. How fed up I am!

One faint hope, one slight, faint hope shines through all this: in every office, especially Mr Nightingale's, girls type away at unimaginable speeds. These last few days in my leisure moments I have set about teaching myself to type. I don't find it easy. Mr Nightingale to whom I mentioned it this evening, told me that it would take me a week.

Then, all at once, he asked me: 'In a week's time when you've learnt how, how would you like to type letters and cards for me in my office?' I said yes, so that's that. As put out as I am to be landed with the postal job, is he going to offer me this quieter work? Or, on the other hand, is he going to add it to my postal job and increase my wages in consequence?

At any rate I cling to a faint hope.

It's getting later. I'm very tired. I'd love to tell you all about this afternoon, the green foliage, the banks of the Thames adorned with dream-houses, the gardens of Hampton Court where there are fantastic flower-beds, long, sanded avenues, well-trimmed lawns that have been mown for the last three hundred years and where whiffs of sweet-scented heliotropes drift across.

But I'd rather keep all this back for later when I can choose my words with more care, express my feelings at a more leisurely pace — rather than going at it full tilt — so that I can describe these gardens in a style that has some literary pretensions.

I'm glad you are concerned about Rivière. He and Guinle have passed the written exam. I am anxiously waiting for a card from them, perhaps a telegram, announcing the result of the oral that ended yesterday. A few days ago Rivière hinted in a brief note that he entertained high hopes. You were very unfair to him last holidays. He combines a first-class intellect with an iron will and a spirit of the kind you rarely encounter more than once in a lifetime. Guinle, more extrovert, is inferior to him in every way, not least in forcefulness of character, but, although at first sight he looks like Lespicier, I'm sure you'll take to him when you get to know him. Guéniffey, who is more on my level, failed his entrance exam by three marks.

Either Isabelle has received my two postcards of last week — in which case it is unkind of her not to have carried out my requests — or else her headmistress is a pig. It is the second occasion when she has withheld the postcards which it is her *moral duty* to hand her.

As my letter must be yet another blow for you, I want to end my Sunday and my letter by trying to cheer you up a bit. Apart from my preoccupations with the language, I live here for the most part in the past. I re-live all my memories. I keep reading through the small bundle of letters that I've kept. The other day, I was reading one from Le Quéré: 'That day we played "stones" at Taro's expense. He's not yet recovered from it . . .' etc. I don't recall what *pion* Taro looked like,[1] but I remembered what 'playing stones' was and I laughed out loud. The rag involves a class of forty boys *suddenly* laying their heads on their exercise-books, each on this desk, so that all the *pion* sees is forty skulls, forty *stones*. Of course it all has to wind up with detentions, but the thing is you've made a *pion* furious and embarrassed! I also remembered what we used to call the *coup de g(râce)*. I've seen it worked on Taro and a brute nicknamed Frère Isambart. We didn't like him: that particular evening in preparation, volunteers, bold spirits, very genuinely busy working — and looking the part — suddenly shouted in turn and without pause in the silence of the study-room, in a voice that went right through you: 'Isambart!' I never saw anyone caught, and it was a splendid rag. Brest was the most studious and the most undisciplined lycée in France. Is that news to you? We carry on in a totally different way at Lakanal. Recently, between the written and oral examination, pupils — having caught the taste from my previous year's commentary — passed round a number of amusing, interesting and witty notes. Guinle had sent one round prophesying everyone's future profession: Guinle himself was to end up, I believe, as a tenor in some lyric theatre, Rivière as music critic of the *Mercure* and myself as a lecturer to women!

Love to you all, in French on the recto, in English on the verso. It is late, I'm feeling tired and a little less perturbed by my present embarrassment of having 'gassed' to you for such a long time.

Kisses,

Henri

P.S. I've adopted this thin notepaper for letters for abroad. This last week I've made amazing strides in English. It happened all of a sudden.

Today, in an out-of-the-way corner of the park, I understood a conversation between Mr Nightingale and a Lancashire gardener from beginning to end. Understanding a conversation you're not taking part in is the most difficult thing of all.

This paper is ghastly but it's torn out of the notebook which you plundered so often. I'll write you a *really* long letter when I'm accepted at the Ecole Normale. For the moment, it is all I can manage. I am merely somebody who for the last six months has been hoping it will be granted to him to scrape through his oral and who can neither work, sleep, nor *sing* nor do anything at all! I'm in an abysmal mental state. And this evening I'm studying French with a frightful headache, a partial blockage in my left (sinister)[1] ear and an awful cold in the head. I don't think I'll ever forget the week that has just ended and the one just beginning. A letter from you would buck me up. I'm very despondent. I promise you a lengthy epistle before 5th August.

A. Guinle

The above is from Guinle, 'Guinle of the Latin epithets' — 'classical' and 'important'.
I. 'sinister' from the Latin 'sinistra' (which means 'left'). Birds of ill-omen passed by on the left — hence our French expression 'sinistre'.

---

1 *Pion*: argot for 'maître d'études' or 'surveillant', responsible for discipline in a lycée.

30 July 1905   *Bordeaux*

My dear Henri,
    Guinle is admitted tenth, Gotteland fifteenth. I am placed
thirty-sixth. I fail to make the Ecole by four places.[1] I'm not
dwelling on it for the moment. You will realize how very upset
I am. My oral wasn't bad, but I failed the written part.
    I haven't the slightest idea as to what I shall do. I'll write
again shortly. I ought to have sent this card from Paris (which I
left last night) but after buying my ticket I hadn't a sou left.
    More fully then, within a week.

                                                                Jacques

P.S. It is practically certain that I've left Lakanal for good, and
Paris for Heaven knows how long!
    Guinle will be writing to you and asking for things.

1   The Ecole Normale Supérieure (ENS) entry is by scholarship examination, and at that time was limited to the first thirty-three candidates each
year.

[postmarked] 1 August 1905

Guinle is placed tenth at the Ecole Normale, though he didn't
do a stroke of work the whole year. Rivière has failed to get in
by four places. He is thirty-sixth, has a bursary for the degree
course and is heartbroken. Guinle is twenty-one years old,
Rivière nearly twenty. Rivière is heartbroken but will be a
success none the less.
    Isabelle, *on the contrary*, is very nice. I've no idea if they will
respond to her Theodore de Banville which Papa alone has
appreciated, but my kisses by way of thanking her.

                                                                   Henri

Written on a postcard of Hogarth's house at Chiswick, which Fournier has
annotated: 'Hogarth: English painter, XVIII'.

Hogarth's House, Chiswick

Guinle est reçu 10: à l'école normale et n'a rien fait de là-bas.
Reçue échoue pour 4 places. Il eut 36°, Gavron 20 bière et nave?
Guinle a 21 ans.
Reçue est nave.
x x Isabelle est, au
contraire, très gentille.
Je ne sais pas si on
refera de son
Théodore de
Banville
que

Rivière près de 20.
mais arrivera   fout de même

Seul le papa a agréé ice, mais moi je l'embrasse très fort pour la remercier.
Hogarth: lecture anglais. XVIII.

110
Henri

2 August 1905

My dear Jacques,

In your next letter . . . which I trust will be long and more cheerful — the exact, new address of *L'Ermitage*, please. Should you have any advice to give me on the subject, let me know.

As for your failure, remind yourself that 'we see only the reverse side of our destiny', for it is merely a matter of fate since you worked harder than anyone else and you failed by only four places!

Decide quickly what you intend to do and, as the English say, *enjoy* your vacation all the same.

Henri

Ask Guinle and Guéniffey to pass on 'things' to you.

4 August 1905

I beg to acknowledge you the receipt of one letter, with accompaniment, of one postcard and of one house.

Henri

Postcard of Trafalgar Square, marked 'near the National Gallery', written in English. (See p. 87)

4 August 1905   *Bordeaux*

My dear Henri,

I can't claim to have a cheerful letter for you, since I was never un-cheered. Here is the whole truth: I was very put out on two different occasions:

1. Immediately after reading the List. Duration: about three minutes. A bottle of champagne to which the lucky candidates treated me put the whole thing out of my mind for that evening.

2. The evening of the following day just as I was leaving Paris. I had in fact no idea when I should be coming back, and that seemed very hard to bear. Into the bargain, I found myself without a sou to pay for dinner, and the emptiness of my stomach added to that of my mind, produced some gloomy reflections. Duration: roughly two hours, thirty-three minutes.

After that, I discovered that I was unusually cheerful and if I hadn't had to cope with my parents' unreasonable obstinacy, I would have cheerfully accepted my fate. But unfortunately I've had to put up with a deal of argument, which I still can't hope to have settled. Naturally everyone is sorry not to see me a *Normalien*. They wanted to persuade me to start another year at Lakanal; that, believe me, I'll never do of my own free will. I've still to recover from nightmares on the subject, but I'm managing it. And a letter from little Bernès — who has proved himself very kind on this occasion — seems to put a very favourable complexion on the affair. In fact, the said Bernès betook himself to the ministry where they held out 'the possibility of the contingency' of some degree bursaries, awarded for the Sorbonne. Of course there's no counting on it, but Bernès wouldn't have volunteered the information without due consideration. There must therefore be an element of truth in it. So, now I am number four and I have sponsors. That's how it stands.

I imagined this letter was going to remove all the difficulties that my parents raised and that they would be satisfied to see me pursuing my studies in Paris. Far from it. They're still hesitating between this and the other bursary for Lakanal which Bazin has renewed. They have written to Bernès to ask his advice. On the quiet I too have written him a longish letter, begging him to give full backing to my cause. He is intelligent enough to see which is the most sensible decision to make. In addition, I wrote a long letter to Mélinand yesterday, telling him about my plans. I found it a rather moving experience,

75

since for the first time, I was setting down in precise terms what I would like to do. It was a twelve-page letter, and I await his reply.

I have often outlined my intentions to you. In a few words I'll summarize what I said to Mélinand. I want to do philosophy and I want to do music; I want to do musical philosophy or even create musical philosophy. I find it slightly embarrassing to explain to you what that means since my own notions of the subject are inevitably rather vague and I need to acquire a great deal of knowledge before I can describe them. But the aim of my work will emerge from the work itself. My work will be to discover exactly how philosophy can be applied to music, to create musical aesthetics, a science of music. If I knew at this moment what this science would be, I would merely have to fold my arms and sit back. For the present then, I am unable to enlarge on it. You'll see what I aimed at when it's done. It may be in fifty years' time; I've no idea. I shall work to the end and I will discover . . . what I discover. If I discover nothing, at least I shall have attempted a worthy and maybe a very useful work.

Practical conclusion: I don't need the Ecole. If I had managed to get in, it would have given me pleasure and have been useful. But I haven't and if I can stay in Paris, the conditions for my work will be no less favourable. I can even make a start in Bordeaux where I shall be serene and undisturbed. Later, if necessary, I'll take a job as a *pion* so as to 'swot' for my P.C.N.[1] and philosophy entrance exam. 'What presumption!' I can hear you say. 'Has he the right mentality for philosophy? His thought process is so slow, diffuse, fragmentary. He is so lacking in Mélinand's power of synthesis. When all is said and done, he is so literary!' It is precisely because I said all that over to myself and panicked at the last moment that I wrote to Mélinand to ask his advice, not so much about my plans as about the quality of my mind. I told him quite frankly the qualities and defects I could discern in it and asked him whether, notwithstanding, I was capable of achieving anything.

But his reply would have to be very discouraging to make me abandon my plans. It's not a sudden flash in the pan. I have pondered over it, weighed it all up for a long time. The 'hénaurme'[2] — hernormous task I have set myself, does not

frighten me. I know that I shall have to study:
1. Philosophy ⎫
2. Music   ⎬ of all three of which I'm sublimely ignorant.
3. The Sciences ⎭
But I'll learn them. Nor is it an idle boast. I am completely confident about what I can do.

Thus I require — and will move heaven and earth to get it — my degree bursary. One more year of boarding school would only arrest my intellectual development. I've extracted every ounce from the teaching of 'advanced rhetoric'. 'Aurrerà' (forward) as they say in Basque, and, by all that's holy, I am here in this world to do something, perhaps!

※

This will serve as a transition. I am going through a period when I'd like everybody to do something. You included! Address of *L'Ermitage*: 38 rue de Sèvres, Paris. You've not heard or received a word about it, I suppose? Well, it can't be helped. You'll have to manage somehow. But how? I've no very clear idea, but manage you must. You have already made an excellent start by going into voluntary exile in England. Go on! Do a great deal of hard work in the 'dump' next year. If you fail, give up the Ecole Normale idea. Take up anything. It's rather vague advice, it's up to you to translate it into action and look around. You must not waste your time getting your name known, you must make every effort to do so. But, if you don't manage this, go ahead anyway, to such effect, through your work, as to gain the strength that will enable you to succeed. This is all very vague, I know, but it's only a general line for you to follow.

For the moment, if *L'Ermitage* doesn't want your poems, ask for them back and try to get yourself known through your prose articles. I think they are easier to place.

I'm not hiding from you the fact that I shall probably be making a similar approach. During these holidays I'm considering setting down on paper one or two of the stray ideas that are wandering in my cerebral convolutions and submitting them — heaven knows where — perhaps to the *Mercure*. It is a necessary step in order:

1. To prove to my parents that you don't have to be a *Normalien* to get into print.

2. So that, in due course, my name won't be completely unknown if and when I come to launch a book. On the whole a review that has accepted you continues to back you later. It is something worth bearing in mind.

But I shan't be accepted. I'm not even sure that I am going to send even the most trifling item to anyone.

For you it's a different matter and much more urgent. Use every possible means to get yourself into print — without, of course, wasting all your time in futile efforts. But insist and persist. There are so many periodicals. It is certain that you'll be accepted by some. The most accredited will take note of your name.

I've bought a postcard of the picture by Jean Veber as well as some Renoirs, a Charles Cottet, a Cazin, a Gustave Moreau and Whistler's *Portrait of his Mother*. They serve as reminders.

*

LITERATURE. I would like to read the whole or part of: Ibsen: *Solnes*, *The Wild Duck*; D'Annunzio: *Les Victoires mutilées*. Yesterday I read *La Giaconda* which I'll talk to you about again.[3] *La Domination*, *Le Triomphe de la mort*. Some Barrès, Wells, Villiers de l'Isle-Adam, novels by Régnier, Paul Adam — *Bruges la Morte*[4] — *Les Surhumains* by Emerson, Carlyle's *Sartor Resartus* and *Heroes and Hero Worship* (please talk about these last two books to find out what the English think of them). Finally, some Leconte de Lisle.

I also want to read Camille Mauclair's *De Watteau à Whistler*, some Anatole France and some Maupassant.

I've bought *Les Jeux rustiques* and *La Sagesse et la Destinée*.[5] Tell me if you've taken with you the *Mélanges posthumes* or some book by Francis Jammes. I will buy the other (*Deuil des primevères* or *Triomphe de la vie*).

Guéniffey has bought *Les Forces tumultueuses*[6] which gives every promise of being a masterpiece.

I will now buy a copy of the *Mercure*. I've been so busy I didn't think of it before. Forgive me if it reaches you a little late this time. I can't locate Chesneau any longer.

I'll stump up for you.

I'll tell you shortly about the *Intégralistes*, a group of young poets who want to replace defunct Symbolism. An interesting bunch.

Yesterday I read a little of André Gide's *Prométhée mal enchaîné*.[7] I have to confess I didn't understand a word. I'll try again.

I think we failed to appreciate Villiers de l'Isle-Adam, perhaps a genius. I'll talk to you further about him.[8]

❊

Please, please forgive me. I thought you hadn't won your gymnastics prize so I didn't claim it. I see from the prize list that you have. Do forgive me. I am a naughty boy. As for myself, I believe I've won six prizes, including the one for philosophy that Mélinand awarded me, I can't think why.

I'm picking up some notions of English — precious few! Write to me. I'll close now. Write to me!

Your *Jacques R.*

No time to read through again. Write to me: Chez Monsieur Fermaud, Domaine de Saint-Victor, Cenon-la-Bastide, près Bordeaux.

In the *Revue des Deux Mondes* there are some very fine verses by the comtesse [de Noailles].[9] I'll transcribe some for you.

1   P.C.N.: Physics, Chemistry, Natural History examination.

2   'Hénaurme': 'enorme', lifted from Alfred Jarry's *Ubu roi* (1896), which abounds in similar humorous distortions.

3   Three of Gabriele D'Annunzio's plays were translated into French under the title *Les Victoires mutilées: La Gloire, La Ville morte* and *La Giaconda*. *La Domination* and *Le Triomphe de la mort* are novels by D'Annunzio.

4   *Bruges-la-mort* (1892), the best-known novel of Georges Rodenbach (1855–98), associate of Verhaeren and Maeterlinck.

5   *Les Jeux rustiques* (1897), poems by Henri de Régnier (1864–1936); *La Sagesse* (1898), essays by Maeterlinck.

6   Poems by Emile Verhaeren (1855–1916), published in 1902.

7   Gide's farce in which Prometheus is caught up in the games of Zeus, 'le banquier'. It was eventually through Gide that Rivière gained a foothold in the *Nouvelle Revue française*.

8   Comte de Villiers de l'Isle-Adam (1838–89), best known for his visionary drama *Axël*. See letter of 18 August.

9   Comtesse Mathieu de Noailles (1876–1933), who belonged to the poetic group known as 'la Nouvelle Pléiade'.

7 August 1905

My dear little Isabelle,

I've just got back from the Tate Gallery and the centre of London where I've spent the whole afternoon . . . Tonight, end of the holiday. We've had the whole of Monday as well as Saturday afternoon and Sunday; it's what they call 'Bank Holiday Monday'. Each season has a similar public holiday . . . So I'm back from the Tate Gallery which I had already visited yesterday — it is a long, long way off in London, by the Thames. I heard the chimes of six o'clock struck at the ancient and sumptuous Westminster Abbey — of which I sent you a view — and I returned home, that is, I took a host of small multi-coloured omnibuses, each sporting a little Union Jack on the top — a host of small omnibuses with a conductor on the step calling out a string of names I still picture, they too, with their stripes and flags, 'Piccadilly Circus! Charing Cross! Tottenham Court Road!' A succession of small omnibuses at one penny, tuppence or threepence a ride, 'buses' to use the familiar expression, which brought me back here at nightfall.

It was understood that this evening I was to 'have tea' on my own. The Nightingale family *was out*. I have just had a little dinner — need I say more, stuffed myself with it. Ah! and with what, you ask? Well, slices of bread and butter, stewed cherries with some kind of jelly, honey, a slice of fruit cake — all washed down with tea with milk. It's just by way of letting you know that one gets used to anything. When I got back, all these small items were on the corner of a large white tablecloth in the room, already dark, that gives on to the lawn and garden — a richly embroidered napkin spread over everything. In the kitchen, next door, three steps to descend, the kettle was standing ready on the gas-ring. It only needed a match to be struck for everything — as in Dickens — to start 'singing'. It did. I went back, kettle in hand, to pour the contents into the tea-pot. Oh! what a comic still-life it formed: the honey in a glass jar on a yellow embroidered doily; the butter too; four tomatoes — which I left — likewise on a glass dish; my two small coloured side-plates, one for the bread, one for everything else; and the saucer on the right between the Chinese teapot and, on a small wooden platter, bread in the shape of a brioche — I got it all down, and, without the fear of the slightest stomach upset! Now, as I am very weary, comfortably installed in my small, green-and-white room on the second floor, the gas light above my head and the blue night glimpsed through the little lace curtain on the right, I feel drawn to the sybaritic life: I have put a top-coat on my seat and draped my jacket over the chair-back. I have chucked my gloves and felt hat carelessly on the table to give myself a sense of luxury combined with comfort.

Dotted about on the table, nicely bound books, a pretty little paper-knife. With all these knick-knacks around me, tired and leaving out an 's' every other line, tired and sleepy, tired but not despondent, tired — yet still writing to you.

✻

The asterisk dividing the letter into paragraphs is an epistolary innovation of Jacques Rivière's. I was hoping for a letter from him this morning, and by the only delivery there has been these last two days, I did receive one — fourteen pages long — from him. It is a model of energy, nay, audacity — precision and clarity. It is really admirable. There's no other word.

On the very morning of his failure by four places, he shapes his life and ambitions. Steps are being taken in Paris at this very moment to ensure that there'll be at least five or six bursary-holders for the bachelor degree, of whom he would be one. Even if he has to take up his bursary in Bordeaux, his life and ambitions are decided. He is taking on an enormous task to start with, and without any display of false modesty, seems to be making a good bid towards its realization. The rest is dream, ambition, maybe genius — maybe fame. That is the dream, and, if things go right, he has convinced me — now that he has allowed me to catch a glimpse of it. He's settled with Monsieur Mélinand in a long letter two days ago, in which he asked advice about setting his course in the way one addresses inquiries to one of the rare, possibly the sole really intelligent man one has ever encountered. He is endeavouring to define the strengths and weaknesses of his mind by asking the teacher he has had now for two years to enlighten him and guide him in his quest; he is not afraid to discuss his ambitions at a time when Monsieur Mélinand is busying himself wherever there are signs of genius, has a hand in everything and applies to it, as Rivière says, 'his extraordinary gift for synthesis', and moves among the élite of the intellectual world. I'll give you a slight idea of what Rivière wants to do; first he intends to take his bachelor of arts degree, his P.C.N., that is, in his case, bachelor of science. He is beginning to study harmony, that vast subject, aiming at the fellowship in philosophy — and that's just the preliminaries, and his dream with all that is to study, perhaps initiate the philosophy of music.

I have no right to expand on it further. All this from one who is his friend and therefore has no call to exercise the caution he himself exercises, must seem, I suppose, presumptuous, over-enthusiastic, ill-considered . . .

I'm sorry I can't send on his letter. The reason is because I know grown-ups hate to hear mere youngsters talk like mature men. And I'm not sending it because part of the letter is devoted to me, to my future, which doesn't concern anyone else — yet.

Monsieur Bernès is very busy getting Rivière to Paris. May all the Bernians be successful this year, hopefully not wafted on vain hopes. Then perhaps 1906 will see our dreams sprout wings. (*Les Ailes du Rêve*, published by Monsieur Bernès, aged about 21, when he was not yet a member of the Upper Council of Public Education — a total literary failure which it poisons his modest existence to recall.)

☀

My friends refer to my stay here as 'your voluntary exile in England, your courageous, laborious initiative, starting-point, etc.' Entreat mama, therefore, not to force me to devote two whole pages of my letters demonstrating and proving that progress in a language, a spoken language, cannot be measured, that you learn only an infinitesimal part in school and that a vast knowledge is required of those who intend to teach it.

Let her not forget that my idea of learning a little bit each day here is what keeps me going; and that she is still further off the mark when she talks about accent, since it is precisely in that area that I had the least need to improve.

On a less dramatic note, I am dealing with another question that mama has raised — twice, three times I let it go, but the fourth time I must protest! Do my feet, draped with their normal coverings — shoes and socks — leave or not leave a nauseating smell in the rooms where they've been? For the last eighteen years, have I been, without knowing it, like Jacques Vinctras, an object of disgust to my fellow men? I agonize as I put down these two question-marks.

As for the letter in which mama, for the last time to date, has raised this question, I confess that I haven't filed it among my valued documents — and in the event of its 'being considered' for publication in a newspaper or periodical . . . I should prefer her to choose another part of our correspondence. One has one's pride, for heaven's sake!

✼

A money matter. Thank 'all at home' as Marie Aufils used to say, and — if God grants her life — still says; thanks very much for the money-order. Give them all a kiss from me, you who know what it is to be short of pocket money to buy oneself the four o'clock snack and coloured chalks. Just bring to their notice that:

1. 20 frs = 15 shillings and a few pence.

2. That since they sent this money-order to *London* instead of to Chiswick, London, I was obliged to go to the Money-Order Central Post Office, London, N, which cost me a mere 12 sous = one sixpence.

3. My *strict* expenses (not a ha'penny less) per week (bed, board & *laundry*) amount to 3 shillings. If the money-order was to cover a month, it would be 3 × 4 = 12 shillings, which leaves 12 sous (sixpence) a week to play the young-man-about-town. It's a temptation, as one person said! It's a 'fiction', as the headmaster at Bourges used to say in his thick local accent. Tell them it all — omitting the thick speech — that wouldn't do! — but in good part, because it is very nice of them to bleed themselves like this for our sake, for us; I say 'nice' in its full implication of goodness, generosity, kindness that we lend the term among friends.

For the first time, I'm typing my bills.

On Sunday morning I paid a visit to the greenhouses, gardens and an area of the vast park of the Rothschilds in London.[1] The same thrill as I felt for Hampton Court gardens, with the additional luxury that such private estates, bath establishments in gardens etc. offer. We owed it all to some estate agent. These conservatories and gardens are reputed to be 'the finest in the land'. I have viewed them but *this evening* I don't feel equal to giving you a detailed account. I saw Japanese gardens, South African hothouses — small orchids at £50 sterling apiece, grapes like those in the Land of Canaan, flower-beds stretching as far as the eye can see, perfumes to make you swoon — ruins on the skyline, ivy-mantled like ancient churches; as a matter of fact they *are* ruins of churches — ancient walls covered with flowers; bamboo bridges everywhere, sand, lilies, geraniums, long gravelled drives; lawns, oak-trees, small rose-clad cottages in secluded corners where people come to spend an annual *fortnight* — and, hidden away in the gardens, pavilions which are bathing-pools, shadowy, where you descend marble steps among the foliage, the rubber-plants and the sea-shells, to a marble floor. Then the arbors, arches, hanging-flowers, paths vanishing into the distance, others leading off behind walls like those of vicarage gardens to strawberry-beds, cloches, peaches, raspberries. Then the park, the deer, the drives, a rusting croquet-set. And yet, it leaves you with a touch of sadness, a touch of ambition. So much richness, poetry above all, for those I do not know and on whom perhaps it is wasted. So much poetry for a fortnight of their lives, and the rest of the time for the gardeners . . .

But, come now! I have told you, haven't I, about the Rothschild expedition — or at least all the impressions that still remain with me at this hour of night as I doze off.

I see that you are starved for music. I ought to have sent you some from Paris. I ought to have. *I would have, I should have!*

Sing the *Ronde*, I'm glad you appreciate it, for your own private and personal pleasure and try not to miss a pause or a sigh. It is full of minor effects which must make their impact without 'hampering' the dance.

Nos coeurs, et vos jupes s'envolent

These little pauses, this little whirling skip — isn't it all charming? And the *on tournera jusque . . . avec la belle que voilà?* Sing the *Ronde!*[2]

I've won a prize for gymn and I insist on collecting it. I think it would be a good idea for you to ask for my school things — that is, what is left of them — at Lakanal. There's always some looking over and mending to be done. Then, in an offhand way, ask for my prize. I'm very proud of it. It seems a bit ridiculous, but what of it! In any case, there's no such thing as ridicule, you are only ridiculous when you're dying of fear for being thought so. I have theories on the subject that I haven't time to elaborate on now before returning to bed.

So, you've won six prizes. That's not at all bad. It was very nice of you to send me a list of their titles.

Servitude et Grandeur militaires is lofty, sorrowful, perhaps profound — a very fine work.[3] The rain falling on the trap with the horseman behind at the beginning, is a kind of rough poetry. Then the terrible story of the red seals.

I consider *Dickens*, with Daudet and Goncourt to be the great novelists of the nineteenth century. Dickens should be read in English or a bad French translation.[4] Even in Dickens nothing surpasses the opening pages of *David Copperfield*. As a novel it has, perhaps, no rival. How he adapts the world to this little boy's world and nothing else — to the limits of a little boy's mind, and in such a moving and sensitive manner, is the work of a great artist, a great poet and perhaps a great philosopher.

Guyau's work is highly esteemed,[5] and selected pages from it are being showered on school girls. He is spoken of as of an author who died young, with a future, a conscience and a pure and lofty soul. I've not read enough of it to appreciate him.

'Vauvenargues by someone or other' can never be as good as undiluted Vauvenargues.

Just fancy! Saying like that quite casually: 'also *L'Acordée de Village*, I no longer recall who painted it . . .'. Well, there was Greuze and Diderot and *Les Salons*,[5] *Le Mauvais Fils puni*, *Le Départ du Mauvais Fils* — domestic virtues and all the half-sincere sentimentality of the eighteenth century. Let's consider, mademoiselle, *L'Accordée de Village* or *Un père qui vient de payer la dot de sa fille*. Not over-declamatory and so pleasing. Certainly the father's over-doing it, with his gesture frozen to all eternity: 'I give her to you, I put her in your care', overdoing his little speech.

Indeed, there is also the mother listening to her husband, drinking up his words, and her tender tears withal.

But there is the young bride with her pretty hand on the young man's arm, there's the sister with a gesture no less discreet, the hens and all the rest. Signed Greuze!

I would be really put out if I'd mistaken the picture! . . .

I kiss you only on the understanding that you will kiss grandmama who will kiss papa who will do the same to mama will send the *kiss* back to me, isn't that agreed?   *Henri*

Do you mind rummaging in my trunk and digging out the *most recent in date* of Miss Lilian's letters. Tear out the two or three in French and post them to me. Don't take the book by Charles Dumas, *L'Eau souterraine* that you'll find there too seriously. He is the first to recognize its immaturity, clumsiness and impersonality. Full of promise all the same: *Intermezzo* . . . and other works.

Some day it would be nice to receive — in the box that Chevalier made — a crust of bread, Seignebos's *Histoire, 1715–1815* and a bound Latin book which is in the loft. It would be nice . . .

I did send you a postcard asking you to enlighten me about Mme Martin on the first floor and her acquaintances, and for information about Toulon.

Your good letter gave me a lot of pleasure. The whole family must set to, follow my example and write long letters. 'It doesn't seem so, you know, but there's a great deal of it, and then, it's closely printed!' as a small boy I know said praising one of his prizes.

I am alarmed to discover that our holidays still continue today, Tuesday. My purse! My poor purse and the little omnibuses!

The concierge at Lakanal has had to pay for a number of 5 sous stamps on a letter from you and on one from Le Queré. Please send me some as soon as possible and I'll send them back to him.

Thanks. Kisses.   *Henri*

1   The Rothschild gardens: Gunnersbury Park and Gunnersbury House, two mansions and the estate, were privately owned by the Rothschilds 1889–1925, when entry would have been by permission. The gardens became public in 1926 and the Gunnersbury Park Museum was opened in 1929.

2   'Our hearts and your skirts fly up'; 'We will dance until . . . with that fair maid': a poem by Fournier, set to music by Guinle. He sent it to his family without admitting authorship. See letters nos. 5, 23, 27.

3   *Servitude* . . . : prose work by Alfred de Vigny (1797–1863), based on his experience of war in the Napoleonic campaigns.

4   The first French translation of *David Copperfield* was published in 1851. It was favourite reading in the Fournier household.

5   Marie Jean Guyau (1854–1888), French philosopher.

6   *Les Salons*: art criticism by Denis Diderot (1713–84), one of the founders of the genre in modern times, and an Encyclopédiste.

13 August 1905

My dear Jacques,

At nine o'clock on Monday morning I was expecting a letter from you; at nine o'clock on Monday morning it arrived.

And if not a cheerful, it was certainly a cheering letter. Well done, old man, what decisiveness, what clarity of views, what a rebound after an apparent fall!

I had allowed myself to be caught up again in old despondencies, in the immense melancholy of Sunday in London, followed, on this occasion, by a Bank Holiday, a public holiday which comes round every season; caught up again in what has been called the immense *loneliness* (solitude, or rather 'isolation' of the present writer) of London these days. I had watched these days, more than any other, arrive with terror, since for the last three there has only been a single postal delivery!

Your letter, expected by this post, has come, has sent flying those fits of depression which had attempted their assault on me, has restored — for some months to come — my confidence, enthusiasm and joy.

Thank you, my dear fellow.

✳

B.S.G.D.G. Jacques Rivière and Co.[1]

I had always 'suspected' you wanted to do something outside the 'ordinary run' and combining music and philosophy. I completely share your views about Lakanal, Bordeaux, the degree bursary . . . Your ideal solution, obviously, is taking up the degree bursary in Paris. There you can enjoy the company of young and old, all those spirits who have ventured on a similar path to yours . . .

You've nothing to be frightened of, I think, where your maths programme is concerned. What you need to get up is acoustics, isn't it? But to learn about acoustics, you don't need to be a Poincaré in maths, blow into foghorns, count the vibrations of taut strings, play with little sounding-boards . . . All that, by the way, is interesting but less so than pure mathematics. I dream of the average and extreme ratio and inverse ratio figures of Père Causse, and I envy you.[2] But the

P.C.N., poor thing, is a dreadful bore and I fail to see in what way it can be of any use. The Natural Science part would frighten me particularly. I've never been able to remember the name of a vein, I've always put phosphorus or albumen in the wrong kind of vessels.

Please forgive me for treating it so light-heartedly. But you will certainly be expecting my comments to be puerile on subjects that are alien to me, are of enormous interest, but on which — for further insight — I await your first volumes.

It is also difficult to discuss projects about which I hardly know the first word.

I am waiting to hear what Mélinand will reply with as much eagerness as if my own future depended on it. At one moment I imagine his letter as written with a smile, the next as excessively serious, since, frankly, it is urgent for you to know what course you are to follow, and, as he says, the 'switch-over' must be made now or never. So I am feverishly awaiting Mélinand's reply which is certain to have arrived punctually.

There is a dream. A dream such as no one dares to have and which I no longer dare entertain since the latest, pretty desperate bulletin — here it is: you, with a degree bursary in Paris, working away at whatever you want; myself, at my parents' house, teachers in Paris or in the suburbs. Myself, following perhaps some of your courses, or as a day pupil for a year or two in a Cagne[3] — myself, in Paris, doing what I want to do (I avoid the word 'swotting' out of shame). But, since hearing the latest from our 'sponsors', it is a dream I no longer dare cherish. Guinle's success completed it. It is a pity that Guéniffey — at least for the coming year — has been stopped by his parents. Otherwise, the dream would have been realized.

*

And I now come to my own plans straightaway, vague though they are. I am probably going to talk about myself shamelessly for several pages. Forgive me. Above all, I am anxious to land up somewhere where I will have my keep and earn some money. That is the brutal truth. I think you'll approve. And it wouldn't worry me if the job was exceptionally agreeable.

a) Because I've had enough of being hard up and, after twenty-five years, it would be horrible to have to struggle to make ends meet.

b) For other reasons you can guess.

I'll probably enjoy swotting in the Cagne enormously. My progress in English will boost my morale. And then I've had my fill of being ignorant as I have of being poor, whatever excuses I may plead, whatever the previous circumstances — perhaps independent of my will — which make me *povre de science et de sçavoir* today.[4]

I will enjoy working because I shall feel free in heart and mind. Because I have got rid of whatever made me — certainly through my own fault and for two whole years — the most miserable and wretched of the wretched. All I shall have behind me will be glimpses of a very pleasant and far-off dreams of my own which I shall shape as I wish and which can only give me courage, peace and pleasantness, something of a Mediterranean dream when I turn towards it.

It could be — still on the subject of jobs — that I'll aspire to another post. Assuming that my zest for work continues and that my parents remain in Paris, I might try for the Colonial service. In the first place, English counts enormously. And then at the factory where I am working eight hours a day at stupid little jobs which nibble away at my brain, I've become aware that I'm no more inept at these aforesaid little jobs than the next man, and that the accountancy required for the first exams at the Ecole Coloniale would not present me with any problem. I can only try for it, however, if my parents come to Paris, since I could then attend any course without creating a bother. Otherwise, as I realize, it is impossible for me to change direction again. That swine Bazin!

The posts offered are excellent. Obviously one has to go off to far-flung places, but in exceptionally luxurious conditions — and then, that would perhaps only be for a time; one would entertain a vague hope of getting away . . .

✳

Now I come to my real aims and hopes. Perhaps they will prevent me from working with positions in view which have always stopped me from working — always, that is at Lakanal and Bourges.

No reply from *L'Ermitage*. I've asked my parents to send

stamps which I will enclose in a letter to the periodical, using the excuse of the wrong address on my submission, thus enabling me to ask them to acknowledge if they haven't yet received it — and in the same letter I shall ask them to return the poems if they don't want them and I shall offer to send further poems if they want to see others and also ask them for the address of the London distributor of *L'Ermitage*, whom I've been unable to locate and as a result a 'little correspondence' may bring me some news. It is altogether unlikely.

The letter consists of four, very brief, sentences and the address: 'H. Fournier — 5 Brandenburgh Rd, Gunnersbury, London W.'.

It would be with some reluctance that I should decide to send my two long recent pieces — specifically composed for a future book — to periodicals . . . But to get off the ground, as you would like me to, I must throw out some ballast.

After *L'Ermitage*, I'll try *La Plume* where I have high hopes — next *La Jeune Belgique*, etc . . . Abandoning *L'Ermitage* will mean, as you know, throwing out much, much ballast.

I earnestly beg you to write the prose you are turning over in your mind. One must try it out a little bit on the left, a little bit on the right before forging straight ahead. People like Camille Mauclair did a bit of everything before becoming the eminent critics that Jehovah created. You can stride out for a long time and very effectively with your music philosophy in your head, or even discover it step by step, arrive step by step to what you will write eventually, even if that seems rather a side issue at present.

I earnestly beg you too not to end your paragraphs 'crowned with confidence' with dispiriting phrases — relics of the feebleness and diffidence of the old school: 'But I shan't be accepted, and I don't even know whether . . .'. It is quite enough that you and I think it, or rather fear it, without your having to say it.

But, without being a professor of stretcher-bearing, *I am in a hurry* to get back to whatever remains of my old plans so often dispersed, upset, fragmented, to whatever is left of their corpses, their ashes, whatever remains today of the faint smoke of their ashes, smoke, alas, just smoke.

From my earliest childhood days in the country, nights in

the dormitories, the plan took shape in my head, the plan I didn't even dare admit to myself — to become a writer. The strange thing, however, is that at first, I did not consider myself *capable of* writing poetry, and, even now, that my grand plans are not to be a poet but a novelist.

Well, the horrid truth is out!

Of course, as in everything else, indeed much more so, you are a man only on condition that you take up your pen to try and say something *different*.

Several times you've heard me speak with a smile about a possible novel: 'Il était une bergère' or suchlike.[5] I have carried this novel around in my head for years, actually less, for three at the most. To start with it was just ' ', 'I', and 'I'! but gradually it began to be depersonalized and no longer the novel that every eighteen-year-old carries round in his head. It spread its wings and now it is becoming fragmented and turning into *novels* in the plural, and now as I am beginning to write the first pages, I seriously wonder if I have anything new to say. Then, seriously, it occurred to me to discuss it with you; not to ask your advice — I find it impossible to hope that anyone can channel the thoughts that arise from the inmost, remotest depths of my being — but to try and talk it over with you a little, explain to you what I mean by the novel, to discuss the *Novel* in general with you.

Walking along one of these streets in the suburbs of London which are like country lanes with so many *châteaux de Sologne* — or elsewhere — but set close together, you can feel very moved, sit on the kerb of the deserted pavement and write the novel which could be taking place at the door facing you. Yes, but what is your material for writing this novel? As you used to say last year, we've had enough of psychological truths and other humbug in the Bourget vein.[6]

As I cast round, I've discovered three categories of response to the challenge: the Dickens, the Goncourt, the Laforgue way.

1. You can write Stories and nothing but Stories. Beginning with one house, ending with another and passing through fields, streets, or sailing in boats, but with just that material at the start and marching ahead with that and nothing else. I mean leaving out of it your own and the reader's personality — joys, memories, and sorrows — and creating a world out of whatever

material you have, but limiting every joy, sorrow, memory strictly to this material. I've put it badly. It will become clearer as I go on.

In *David Copperfield*, for example, you come into the world with him and if you find yourself desperately sad in chapter 7, it is because you are so far away from the house introduced in the opening pages. In chapter 5, the small boy is exiled to a boarding school in London to which a poor, young assistant master takes him. They stop for a meal with some poor women, one of whom is the assistant master's mother. The boy falls asleep to the sound of a flute which the master has produced to soothe the old woman who is utterly disagreeable, ridiculous, atrociously ridiculous.

Yes, but at Salem House, later, as a consequence of an indiscretion on the part of the small boy, a 'big boy' treats the assistant master condescendingly as a beggar and gets him sacked. The undermaster puts up with all the arguments and insults as he stands with his hand on the shoulder of the small boy who had come up to his desk to ask a question, and, in the evening, the small boy who usually recounted stories to the big boy and others in the dormitory, is unable to do so that evening and then, finally, when he has succeeded in getting them all into bed, he seems to hear the flute of Mr Mell, the poor assistant . . . sounding so plaintively . . .

The chapter goes on, life goes on and, like the world, keeps on turning. Yet, at every moment, since it is the small boy who is telling his story, the world of the book is limited to the world of this little boy, a world as perfect of its kind, evidently, as Mélinand stated, as any other world — but it is still only the world of this small boy.

You live with him — you have to live his life, watch life go on around him and every means is used to make it live: twitches, grimaces or tears — you have to live them. His world must exist, but your knowledge will be limited to what has happened in that world, its loves, its desires, its sorrows.

That is a very brief and rapid summary, free of any didactic claims, of what I see in Dickens's novels, even his comic novels. (I am not referring to pages in which he has, like anyone else, made concessions to human imbecility which you can find even at the end of *David Copperfield*.)

2. There is the Goncourt way. I hardly know anything of his except *Germinie Lacerteux* but since I consider all that as a preamble to my own case, it will suffice.

Goncourt is already a very different matter. He has collected up everything that offended his hypersensitive sensibility, and, without over-much attention to writing a real story, a simple story, he rams it all into his novel. Everything he has seen, everything simple, moving, wretched and sordid that he has found in the woman of the people, he pins on to Germinie Lacerteux. All of this he divides into small chapters which could be labelled: Melancholy of the Streets, Melancholy of the Cemeteries, Monstrosity of the Fortifications, the Night Dance-Halls, etc. . . .

Certainly, it is also an important study of the effects of love and vice on a candid, passionate soul of 'a woman of the people', in Paris. If you like. But what I have seen in it above all is what I am telling you: a hotch-potch of sensations, predominantly the author's, tagged on to a character who is secondary and no more than secondary.

3. With Laforgue, total absence of characters; he couldn't care less about them. He is himself at once author, character and reader. The character embarks on a boat one August evening: Ah! twilit evenings over little bridges in summer; ah, the swallows in flight, dogs barking over their bowl on a barge at its moorings. Come, come, that's enough: the character is now in the spring sunshine. Ah! these mornings such as no longer exist, with bees in the grass, etc . . .

It is, granted, more real, more profound than reality. There's no cheating, nothing anecdotal about it. But *it is no longer a novel*, it's something else.

As you observe, I quickly move on to my own case. It is at this point that I become very embarrassed. In spite of myself, meditating as I continue my novel, these individuals sprang to mind, and that is why I have come to classify them in a hundred different ways, of which this is the last.

You can be sure that I didn't start out from these three or four theories in order to arrive at a fourth or fifth of my own and set down the subjects and paragraphs to fit in with the theory.

My novel is in front of me, being transformed as it progresses; the 'Faguets'[7] will follow later; I am only doing my little 'Faguet' exercise to give you some idea of the novel itself without attempting to categorize it.

I started with the idea of introducing my theories on philosophy, love and society into it . . . Later, it occurred to me to narrate my own stories, just mine alone, with my own memories, to write a poetic autobiography. People always have ideas more or less on these lines when they want to write, only, there are scores of ways of holding them.

At present I would favour the Laforgue pattern, but applying it to a novel. But it's a contradiction in terms; if one turned life with its characters, the novel with its characters, into a mere series of dream-encounters, it would no longer be a novel. I use the word 'dream', irritating and threadbare as it is, for convenience. What I mean by dream is a vision of the past and its hopes, a reverie of former times renewed meeting a vision that is beginning to fade, the memory of an afternoon as it encounters the dazzling white of a sunshade and the freshness of another experience.[8] As in dreams, things go wrong — there are false trails, changes of direction. It is everything that lives, moves, links up, drifts apart, undergoes change. The rest of the character is more or less routine — social or animal — and devoid of interest.

What I am telling you seems the statement of the age-old, banal truths in a slightly different form.

My aim is precisely to turn this *form*, this way of revealing life into something that can be experienced in novels, and so to work it that this incommensurably rich treasure of accumulated lives which — youthful though it is — compose my simple life, shall see the light of day in this form of walking 'dreams'.

Maybe it will take another shape. I may change. For the moment the aim is, as you see, to suppress characters and the anecdotal, yet still be a novelist — a novelist and above all, a poet.

It's not saying very much, or rather it is saying too much, so much that one gives the impression of having said nothing, and that, after all, becomes everybody's idea.

To finish, like you, on a pessimistic note, I'm not saying that I'll probably write nothing; I am too tempted to write something, but I think that my initial works, against all expectation, including my own, will be sickeningly banal and *déjà lu*, and if I manage to say anything new, it will be after repeating for a long time all the material from various sources that I've sifted and re-sifted.

In the meantime, I just hope I can write somewhat more personal poems and that I have not been too long and boring in my attempted explanation of plans.

N.B. Of course I am not unaware of the talents, even the genius, of a host of other novelists. I have not mentioned Daudet, for example, because he did not seem to me to occupy a well-defined place between Dickens and Goncourt. In my previous classifications, on the contrary, he occupied the front rank.

My final conclusion — arranging my career on your lines — will be, to use your expression, that 'you will see what I was trying to do when it's done', and this applies still more perhaps to the novel than to music — and even if I knew exactly what I want to do, it wouldn't merely be a matter of sitting back with my arms folded.

✻

For the moment, I have sacrificed my Sunday to It and to you. After a cold bath this morning, I tackled your letter; as I got up late, I had to interrupt it in the middle of my 'novel' section to go and have lunch. This will explain, despite the lightness of the aforesaid, the weightiness of what follows.

My hosts have gone off this morning for a fortnight's holiday at the seaside, leaving me at my request, absolutely alone in their house. They've left me heaps of provisions for morning coffee and afternoon tea, and I lunch out.

I was instantly thrilled to have a garden and two floors of the house to myself, to give free rein to my luck and liveliness. But first, it is only for Saturday evening and Sunday. The rest of the time — from 8 till 6! — occupied in tiring work, early bed, exhausted. Saturday and Sunday, in spite of my wish to stay here and busy myself with my day-to-day life, I need to get out. These four walls seem to bear down on me. I need to go out, despite the lack of anything special to do in London and despite all the money you spend there.

At the present moment, I'm taking your letter from my room on the second floor, where it is too hot and there's too much sun, to the dining-room which looks out on to walled gardens full of shade, where I find it too gloomy. I've finally ended up in the drawing-room where, as everywhere else, it's lonely, lonely.

I have become aware that there are limits to human solitude. This morning I became aware that I was no more than a recording apparatus registering new sensations and a repeater of old ones; now and then, at regular intervals, a phonograph repeating expressions heard in a language very different from the wallpaper manufacturer's. That's what it amounts to; I've no life of my own — whether I'm ugly or handsome, well or badly dressed, sad or lighthearted, those around me couldn't care less; as a result, I end by not caring myself either, and then I cease to have a life of my own. It would be ideal for someone who wanted to pause awhile to watch and stare at the past as it goes by; yes, fine if only I had time left over to do that. As it is, it's tough going and I'm afraid of lapsing into bitter melancholy or going gaga.

But that is only an impression of the moment and it's wrong of me to bring it up since I am going to hurry and finish your letter, then sally forth to try and find a French newspaper and after a tonic cup of tea, stimulating and excellent for the grey cells, do a long spell of work by gas-light.

*

I am beginning to realize too that personal letters have their limitations.

I have still more things to write to you about — in future letters:

A chapter about things that have distressed me. You are anxious to destroy my memories of them, but I'd like to discuss them with you in general terms.

A chapter on London.

A chapter on the way all my memories of past holidays, which I am now missing so much, come back to me — all my memories of the countryside, deprived of it as I now am. Over here, I don't really know whether it's the landscape of this or that spot that I am missing, or things past which took place there. It adds up to a very tender and deep emotion which could be called 'nostalgia for the past'.

Thus La Chapelle d'Angillon, where I've spent my holidays for the past eighteen years, comes before me like the place of my dreams, the land from which I am banished — yet I see my grandparents' house as it was in my grandfather's time: that cupboard smell, the creaking of the door, the little wall crowned with flower-pots, peasants' voices — all that life, so special that I would need pages to convey any impression of it. And further, I must confess that, with the excuse of my privations as I sit here in front of English ham and preserves, my thoughts turn wistfully and longingly to the smell of bread delivered at noon, the smell of country cheese at four o'clock, my grandmother's cherry-brandy, all the wholesome smells from cupboards and wardrobes and the garden.

Another land which is that of my dreams, where, for the last eighteen years I always spent a fortnight at the shooting season, is Nançay. At the moment there's nothing I desire more than to go and spend my last week of the holidays at Nançay. That and to be buried there. So far, I have only known the silent happiness of living there. All the poetry — immense — I am not exaggerating, of my life down there, comes back to me at this moment.

It is my father's country. In every field they call him 'Guste' (for 'Auguste') and address him with the familiar 'toi'. It's the country of my cousins, uncles and aunts. You arrive after some five leagues' journey by side roads and in old-fashioned traps. It's a remote region deep in the Sologne; the roads are dry; it is carpeted all along with yellowing pine-needles, bordered with fir woods over the surrounding plains; there are gadflies in the air, game-birds fly across your path. We have endless tales of wrecked carriages, storms, the horse stuck in the mud of some ford where you stopped for it to drink. Add to all this, at the edge of the woods, distant horizons beyond the trees and roads, such as you don't set eyes on by the sea, even at Toulon.

So much for the journey.

In this remote region, Uncle Florent who welcomes us, keeps — strange to relate — a huge general store, divided into departments just like those in towns, to which people come for supplies from a ten-league radius. The manor houses which abound in the Sologne would have been worth a fortune to him long ago — with their custom — but the idea didn't appeal to him. He prefers to have lots of children — only one is a boy — Robert, who is my age.

The house of Raimbault-Fournier which is at the end of a street welcomes us as we emerge from a fir-wood, with a warmth whose sincerity I have never doubted: at the doors and behind the windows uncle with his luxuriant moustache, aunt with the bonnet which she always refuses to exchange for a hat, and her excessively intelligent country finesse (no exaggeration) and her *ten* daughters (no exaggeration!).

I am abandoning any attempt to describe life in this village store. It has always seemed to me, as in *David Copperfield*, a world of its own — all the people who pass by, stop, bargain, all the carts that drive up with the rain dripping off them while bargaining proceeds, all the carriages that have travelled in the sunshine by the Souèsmes road, the fragrant smell of coffee in the grocery; the odours of the hat-room, the boot-room, the oil-room, the umbrella-room — an endless succession of rooms through which I pass, hand in hand with my little female cousins with their comic Souèsmes accent.[9]

Opposite, quite close, a belfry which always seemed to me to ring out cheerfully hours that rushed past but were heard in the distance for some time.

At the back of the store, the living quarters, the kitchen. We have dinner, as they do on farms, in a vast kitchen. All day long different lives go on there side by side, sporting life and family life: children and dogs running around. Florent's brother, Philippe, mustachioed like him, cartridge-pouch and gun between his legs, while he chats or eats and distributes kicks among his dogs. Other sportsmen, and among them all, a heartier good fellowship than anywhere else you can think of. This is amply proved by the mass of food they stuff into you; you never stop eating; at every moment there's a cup of coffee at hand and a rump of rabbit waiting for you. 'Come now, to put some strength into your legs before you go shooting.' 'Robert, pour a drink for your cousin.' 'Henri, little Henri, have I got to go and find Marie-Rose to persuade you to have some more?...'

And then we go shooting in the pinewoods, whole days

among the heather with the uninterrupted crackle of gunshot on every side, the whiff of cordite; lunch, wherever you land up, at the houses of private gamekeepers attached to these Sologne manor-houses, almost each one of which is a wonderful example of perfect taste, elegance and poetry in the midst of rough country.

We come home exhausted. We pass through the store where sales are brisk before dinner-time, on September evenings when the dusk is already lit up by dazzling paraffin-lamps. Tired out, we collapse on to chairs in the kitchen. Here we wait for dinner when the room will ring to the sound of childish laughter — mama joining in madly with the rest — and where our two families alone fill the places at all the tables. The dinner may well be interrupted by my uncle's vans arriving in the dead of night, the dismounting by the light of the lanterns of other uncles and aunts who have been collected up at distant railway stations and whom we are very soon embracing with only a vague idea of who they are. Meantime, the horses are led off to hay-stacked stables which they fill with the steam rising from their coats.

Among the dim candles, to the clatter of dishes, we wait for dinner in the kitchen. We become drowsy. To entertain us they take down from the walls and pass around old smoky photographs. School groups. We see my father, aged five, with Monsieur Jaury, the village teacher who used to beat him so much and who now doffs his skull-cap and greets him with a low bow. We see all the young kids of this school in the old days — the very ones who now call my father 'Guste'.

Well, that's that. I'm satisfied now. I think I've done justice to this chapter.

Listen, old fellow, do forgive me for having indulged in 'literature' for two whole pages on the subject. It was more than I could resist.

Two years ago I brought Jean to spend this annual fortnight at Nançay with me. For me, everything was still the same as it had been eighteen years ago, nothing seemed to have shrunk, except perhaps my cousin who is now a teacher. Once we were on the way I was in the grip of my childhood ecstasies. Jean infuriated me by asking about my handlebars, about the superiority of Peugeots over Cléments. He hadn't a clue about

Uncle Florent, and it's only been recently that he spoke to me about Nançay again and that I felt that, in spite of himself, he still had a soft spot for all this good, gentle way of life.

When as a small child I was coming away from Nançay, I always prayed that some accident on the way would oblige us to turn back; at each of the milestones we passed, I left behind something of myself — and I felt an immense sadness on saying goodbye to Nançay thus, for a whole year, the holidays and the summer.

I am ashamed to have let temptation run away with me and to have recounted to you a thousandth part of what I have to tell. Never before have I spoken to anyone (not even to my parents, on account of certain family differences) about the charm Nançay had for me. It all comes back to me here more vividly than ever, among other recollections, so sweetly melancholy, because I am far away and alone.

All I've been telling you must seem boring and absurd. It would be nice if you who have appeared sometimes to be interested in this kind of very personal recollection — the kind my heart, after all, is composed of — were to consider it neither boring nor absurd.

It is one's dream to find a friend who can respond to one's past, the life of way back and yesterday, who can find it interesting, is eager to be interested in it. Is such a dream possible? I think it is what people look for, above all, in love, and they rarely find it because if there is one 'dream' (or two) which exactly matches your own, there are so many others which fail to, and pass close by yours without stopping. Anyhow, I will return to the theme in a future letter.

In the meantime, I thank you just for the fact that *it is to you* that I've been weak-minded enough to talk about it all.

※

Towards the end of the 'Nançay' chapter I went out for a walk. On my return, I did a bit of this and that, then Mrs Martin who is here only until tomorrow morning, came and asked me to take tea with her and accompany her to church. I did so; only now, as it approaches ten o'clock, am I continuing with my letter.

How sorry I am, my poor friend, for having wasted my time telling you things which are of so little interest to you, and that

I should have to work so hard at to make them interesting, when I had so many more topics of more general interest to relate.

By way of slight compensation this time, I insist at least on telling you that everybody in England knows about Maeterlinck. I am putting it too strongly; he is very well-known. My old ladies know teachers who have talked to them about him as of a great philosopher. Among the newspaper cuttings my young lady pen-friend has sent me (the controversy as to whether or not Emily Brontë wrote *Wuthering Heights*), there is an allusion to Maeterlinck as a great, subtle, profound and well-established philosopher.

They have a rather special attitude to literature here. Everybody laughs at me about Kipling, maintaining his tales are either for 'children' or 'soldiers'.

So, for my future letters I shall have, in addition to the two chapters announced above:

A literary chapter on Kipling, Carlyle, Emerson, Thomas de Quincey, etc . . . (Laforgue lost in transit, I shall buy but later *Le Deuil des primevères* as being the first in date after *L'Angélus*. If you prefer to buy it, do so, but let me know).

A chapter on a visit to Hampton Court — oh! unforgettable — accompanied by two or three supporting engravings; on a visit to the Rothschild gardens, likewise unforgettable, and another to Westminster Abbey which failed to interest me, perhaps because I was tired.

A chapter concerned with art in the Kensington Museum, the Wallace Collection and especially the Tate Gallery (four pages on the Tate). I had been there the day just before the arrival of your letter and I returned enraptured. I was walking on air. I went back the same evening. I have notes, even a sketch, and a list of favourites. I'll write to you about Burne-Jones, Rossetti, *Watts*, Leslie, Walker, Orchardson, Millais, Mason, Graham, above all *Watts*.[10] I had made a mental decision to do it today and I'm sorry to have allowed myself to be side-tracked. I'm eager to send you my sketch, a little thumbnail of an admirable Saint John from an admirable painting by Ford Madox Brown that I came upon.

Then, for future letters, a chapter on the English whom I've ended up liking very much, whom in not a few ways I'd like to resemble and whom in many ways I do. They are very advanced in everything, especially politics, though they keep quiet about it.

About [the first] Yvonne, now that you have reminded me of her, I can tell you that I no longer bear her any ill will and that nothing concerning her at present can cause me either pleasure or pain, and that I don't even owe her any gratitude for having been 'raw material', since it was not *with her* that I found inspiration for 'the work of art'. All that's left is my rather troubled curiosity as to where my prose is at the present moment and where those letters which are neither *of me* nor *for her* are lying around. Have you any idea? In point of fact, those letters in which I tried to be *her* ideal — the whole thing was pathetically stupid — in which I was just myself and nothing else, didn't seem to be addressed to her at all. This is plain to me in the letters I still have, some of which are quite abysmal.

Finally, there will be other chapters that I envisage, but I find it a bore to enumerate now. Please forgive the inordinate length of all that I am sending you. It's become more than a letter. I am so lonely. Having you to talk to has kept me company the whole day.

My other letters will be more reasonable as regards length. I'd like to come to an understanding with you about our correspondence which I would dearly like to be regular, and which in my case will be less gushing, more English, than today's effort.

You cannot imagine how eagerly I am waiting for the *Mercures*: those of 15 July and 1 August. Doubtless no *Ermitage*. For more than a month I've not read anything of all the modern gang who interest us. The other day I was in my seventh heaven as I read 'Sur Mer', the first section of *Forces tumultueuses* that Guéniffey copied out for me. Good heavens, how good it is! Since 1 July I've had the promise from Guinle of a weekly letter which has failed to materialize. Being a *Normalien* doesn't make people punctual.

Eleven o'clock. Goodbye.

Till the next.   *Henri*

---

1 *Breveté sans garantie du Gouvernment*: patent without government warranty.

2   Père Causse: mathematics teacher at Lakanal.

3   *cagne*: class preparing pupils for the entrance examination (*concours général*) for the ENS. Fournier had to repeat his year, but failed also in his second attempt (1907).

4   Adapted from *Le Grand Testament* of François Villon (1461): 'povre de sens et de savoir' — poor in my wits and wisdom.

5   A popular French folksong, here typifying the bucolic approach. The theme did indeed surface in 'The Sheepfold' (I:10) in *Le Grand Meaulnes*. Seen under moonlight, it evoked in Alain-Fournier's mind a recollection of Thomas Hardy, reflected in the style.

6   Paul Bourget, exponent of the psychological novel, e.g. *Le Disciple* (1889).

7   Émile Faguet (1847–1916), noted literary critic and historian.

8   The sunshade is a recollection of his encounter with Yvonne de Quiévrecourt. He mentions it in the letter he wrote to himself (see appendix II).

9   In *Le Grand Meaulnes* III:2, Fournier's uncle Florent and his family are the basis for the characters of Uncle Florentin, Aunt Julie, Marie-Louise; the above description of their store is elaborated in the novel.

10   Most of this painter's works now form part of the Watts Collection, to be seen at Compton, near Guildford, Surrey. The Collection includes those paintings described by Fournier in letter no.30.

23   TO ISABELLE FOURNIER

14 August 1905

My dear little sister,

I am sending you the enclosed because it's so good. I already knew some poems by Verhaeren, in particular the one I read out to you and Papa last Easter, that long, wild, yet divine poem written in alexandrines of portentous power, entitled: 'Les Moines'. At that time I didn't know *Les Forces tumultueuses*. I had no idea he could be so delightful, gentle, so firmly gentle, and, on the arrival of this piece which my friend Guéniffey sent with his last letter, I felt that I could not allow anyone I was fond of miss it. That's why I'm sending it.

Nor will I mind if those at home should gain some faint notion of what these poets whom the insignificant, provincial ladies a decade ago dubbed *the decadents*, really are.

Emile Verhaeren could, in fact, be called a romantic-symbolist. He derives at once from Victor Hugo and Henri de Régnier.

I enclose the piece without further commentary. I know you are intelligent and open-minded enough to grasp the meaning of the whole and realize that there's no such thing as abstract 'truth' in the world, but only those who examine it, seek it out; and that there are a hundred ways of seeing it — and that it is for that reason that poets as different as Jammes, Samain[1] and Verhaeren can each be a great poet in his own way — the first with his simplicity, the second with his remote, ancient visions, the third with his visions of glory and gold and his iron grip. And then, don't you think that when Poetry is achieved, they all come together? And that Verhaeren says things of a simplicity that can move one to tears in the piece I've sent?

Note that they are all — or were, since Samain is dead — close friends.

Note too, the consummate skill of these *vers libres*.

I don't know whether it's because I had not read anything like it for such a long time, but it's certainly a very long time since I was moved so much.

A last goodnight. How beautiful it is!

Henri

[1] I had intended to include as well a piece that my friends like very much, part of which is similarly in *vers libres*, although it is a little too reminiscent of Francis Jammes — by the same author as 'La Ronde', with words that appeal to mama so much.

But, to speak the truth, it pales too much in comparison.

So I prefer to keep the surprise back for another week — if you think it really is a surprise, in other words, if you'd like it.

2. Provided mama thinks you are old enough for me to talk literature with in this way.

I hope so, and I remain

your Henri

To make your mouth water, all through this piece you'll think of Madame Benoist's house. At least it had that effect on me.

By the way, may I send one or two cards to Alfred and

Jenny?[2]

May I send one too to Rabillon who must consider me *very rude* to neglect him?

1   Albert Samain (1858–1900), a poet little influenced by the contemporary *symboliste* and *vers libres* movements.
2   Alfred and Jenny Benoist were childhood friends from Epineuil; Rabillon lived in La Chapelle.

24   TO MARIE AND AUGUSTE FOURNIER
(in English to the sentence 'Please let me know this.')

14 August 1905

My dears,

I hope you have not been too angry with my last letter and it has not been misunderstood like the majority of my poor letters.

You have very well seen that I have only to pay my 'week' before I have received it, haven't you? I hope so, and I leave out this question. But I have intended, today, to settle in English all the annoying questions, so that the remainder can be read by everybody.

As for 'Paris', I am just writing to Jean and asking him to let me know what Mr Bernard thinks about the letter you have received. Is it only the 'official' part of the business, and have we something to hope from the 'officious' department, vis, from the cabinet-heads? At any rate I wonder this affair has not been settled between cabinet-heads, as it had been promised.

I think it would be preferable you write also from your own part to Mr Bernard and explain what you have received, in quoting the names, without any mention of the hopes I gave you, last June. Be patient, perhaps the time of those hopes is not up.

I shall be, this fortnight, quite alone, you know, and impatiently waiting something that can keep me company . . . letters, parcels, books, bread . . . and so on . . .

Your letters are always dreadfully short, they don't really

answer my awfully long letters, and it's not kind of Isabelle not to come more often and cry 'cheer up' to her poor exiled brother. Have a special day for each of your letters, as the Englishmen and I have, think out what you have to say, during the week, and when the special day comes, you will be only pleased to write it down.

As for the parcel, don't forget the books, pray; if not Isabelle, someone can fetch them in my trunk, cannot he? It will be so kind of him or her, Bread is also marvellously waited for — and, as Mr Gauthier had promised me to take to me a trunk of bread, this make[s] me think of him and of his journey. I wonder if they have made up their mind about it. Please let me know this —

They were obliged to take away my typewriter and now that I have to speak in French and tell you things of interest, I find I've nothing much to say.

My dears, first, I'm still waiting for letters from everyone. For the most part, none of you are either energetic or nice; and am I who *cudgel my brains* to find things to interest you!

With this letter I enclose a short one I wrote on Saturday evening for Isabelle and which, alas, must have reached you after the other of more immediate interest. I think you'll find it interesting.

Mrs Martin, a little old lady who lives with her sister on the first floor and only left this morning, invited me to take tea with her yesterday afternoon. She is a school teacher, very affable, absolutely insists on my meeting her nephews and getting away from the company I frequent or rather don't frequent and which moreover is very agreeable. She took me along to the Protestant service at six o'clock, impressive in its simplicity, its convictions and really very beautiful.

I like and greatly admire the distinctive characteristics of the English: reserve, good manners, restraint in speech and behaviour, inner life . . . I have the secret pleasure of finding myself English in some respects. And when one has the opportunity of comparing their behaviour in public transport or elsewhere with that of the French. Great heavens! the comparison is quickly made. I particularly admire their outward demeanour; it brings out their inner life in an extraordinary way.

Furthermore, where politics are concerned, for instance, I am far from saying that their ideas are inferior to those of the French. I am keen to discuss the subject with Monsieur Gauthier. You should see how, alongside reverence for their old things and their ancient customs, they produce theories which are marvels of common sense, or rather, of reason. And you ought to see how they put these devastating theories quite casually into practice.

The other day, I had a long political discussion with Mr Nightingale. We spoke of the death penalty, of crime and of poverty. I should mention that he has his part in the business of this firm which is the first in England and Europe for the quality of their wallpapers; their 'social' innovations, improvements, etc, are imitated by most London companies.

But first I should state that Mr Nightingale (for whom my esteem is not thereby diminished one whit) started there as an ordinary workmen and is now the boss.

In the second place, we discussed these serious questions of Charity, Justice, Alms. I hardly dared to advance those theories — reasonable in all conscience — which say 'Justice first, then charity', or rather, once justice is done, there won't even be any question of exercising charity, and until such a stage is reached, I wouldn't give a fig for all your charities, since even the most sublime would amount only to a tiny particle of fair restitution.

I hardly chanced saying all that. Well, he burst out laughing as he told me the story of a Belgian who came to his house and observed: 'in my country there's a conflict between Catholics and Socialists. But we Catholics will win since *we give most* to the workers.'

When you go into the question, it turns out that this Belgian aristocracy — one of the most unenlightened — goes to any lengths to see that the workers live in neighbourhoods that are furthest away from the town centres, and by cutting their wages to the minimum, are kept half-starving. Then later, with a great play of pomp and ceremony, they distribute alms. 'Why can't they give them the work they ask for, the wages they deserve, let them follow their own way of life, tastes and customs and give them a fair deal and then there would be no need for the rich to visit them and take them food', remarked Mr Nightingale with a hearty laugh. In all honesty, he considered those Belgians unbelievable.

You'd search in vain for a Mr Nightingale among the heads of firms in France.

The main thing is that we saw eye to eye: on the death penalty, etc . . .

I can't help feeling inhibited in these high-speed conversations in which I've to try to avoid making blunders in language and getting hold of the wrong end of the stick.

Yesterday I wrote page after page to Rivière about the Tate Gallery and art in London. He replies with page after page at a fixed day and time.

Last Tuesday evening I was invited to *Supper* at my Spanish friend's [Señor Couchi]. For the last eight months he's been lodging at the house of a young English lady — whose husband is a major in the Medical Corps in India — and her daughter, and lodging so comfortably that he has ended up by becoming engaged to the sixteen-year-old daughter.

From eight to half-past eleven, music; at nine o'clock, supper, that is, a slice of ham and preserves. Quite a crowd there. We play those little parlour games the English adore. Fate ordains that I 'kneel to the wittiest, bow to the prettiest and kiss the one I love the best'. It's embarrassing, for they are all more or less engaged. But I get away with it by dashing straight over to kiss the oldest and most wrinkled lady, to bursts of laughter and cheers from the whole room.

I've been to see Westminster Abbey, but I'll have to go back. I was too tired to appreciate it.

I'll tell you more about my life in the empty house in a few days' time. An engaged couple turn up every evening to get things ready.

I've got used to the food, but I realize I'm in one of the houses where you have most to eat.

Don't forget my stamps.

Love and kisses all round.

Henri

17 August 1905   *Bordeaux*

My dear Henri,

Today, Thursday, 17 August, I am making a start and have no idea when I shall finish. Thank you very much indeed for your time — and please, please, don't make your future letters any shorter. Having said that, I begin:

I. MYSELF. That's not a very modest start, but I like to leave the most interesting item for the end. I've received Mélinand's reply — punctual — despite a slight delay caused by the peregrinations of my letter which only caught up with him in Switzerland. It is very much on the lines I wanted, but as it is impossible to summarize, here it is:

Four lines of sympathy — in firm tones — on my failure. Then:

> You are quite right not to take it too much to heart: it will probably do little damage to your future.
>
> It seems obvious to me that you can and even should 'do philosophy'. The faults you recognize in yourself with a somewhat harsh clarity are those of a young man; not serious and, above all, not irremediable; the qualities we recognize in you are now sufficient evidence of a genuine philosophic cast of mind. So, in principle, the matter is easily resolved. There is certainly the problem of the Bachelor of Science degree, but it's an illusion; you have got it into your head that you do not like the sciences; you will find them engrossing when you go back to them with a slightly more mature approach. No serious difficulty there. As to your special plan about musical philosophy, it is very interesting and feasible: however, there are certain reservations to be stated: first, I do not know whether the plan provides enough material for a whole lifetime; and then it is a less unexplored and virgin world than you think. Dauriac has devoted himself to it; a younger man, Landormy, is taking it up, as are others who have left school more recently.[1] Please note that these are not objections, merely points to be considered. Lastly, you would be forced to defer this project; your admission to the *agrégation* might suffer and even your start

in teaching.[2]

(He is thinking about Landormy who resigned as a teacher to sing in the chorus at the Brussels Mint.)

> You must have the courage to give up music *to some extent* when you are preparing your detailed syllabus for the *concours*.
>
> So much for your long-term future. What must you do next year? My personal feeling is that you have extracted everything you can from the lycée; an additional year would be marking time — in short, a year towards your career wasted. The best thing, if possible, would be to win a bursary for the Sorbonne; I know you are serious enough to work in spite of being a free agent. There is really no longer any special point *now* in your remaining at school and perhaps it is better not to give it another thought.
>
> This, my dear Rivière, is what I believe to be the best advice I can offer you. It is, of course, only one point of view, and you have to take a host of considerations into account. Make a quick decision so that you can enjoy a good vacation which you certainly deserve.

I should add that in my letter I begged him to write me the kind of letter I could show to my parents and use as a weapon. That accounts for the tone, especially that of the last part, written for my father's benefit. Such as it is, I find it encouraging, despite Mélinand's well-known optimism that if he advises me not to worry about my weaknesses and frankly to go ahead, it is because he thinks I've got the guts to do so. I do know that he is incapable of offering such advice without giving it due thought. So I'll do my best to take philosophy. And that is even if I have to remain in Bordeaux — since a young lady from here has come out second in the *Agrégation de Philo*, which gives me more confidence in the Faculty in my native place. Be that as it may, I hope my parents will consent to have a philosopher son instead of an Athenian. It won't be easy, but I'm hopeful.

There's still the question of musical philosophy about which Mélinand voices his reservations. Maybe he's right? But perhaps I am? I'd like to say to him with a faint smile: 'As for that, leave it to me; you'll see. I'm grateful for your advice, but we'll see.' You understand that I want to accomplish something rather more complete, coherent, systematic than what Dauriac, Romain Rolland[3] or Landormy have accomplished. But, as I said, I'm not sure what. But it is something that will (I hope) emerge eventually in the way a mountain looms up as you approach and ascend towards it. For the moment, all I know is the name of the mountain. I shall become familiar with its shape as I climb it. To win your forgiveness for this sustained and over-picturesque metaphor, I'll return to simplicity and say: 'We'll see.' What I gained from Mélinand's 'restrained guidance' is his advice that I should devote myself first and foremost to philosophy and *the sciences*.

It's naturally this *sciences* business that rather worries me, You don't only have, as you surmise, to do acoustics. To do philosophy you must at least have your *bachot*[4] and — I believe — your P.C.N. But, according to Mélinand, the P.C.N. doesn't seem to be required. However, I'm going to inquire as to whether I have to pass my *bachot* before or after my *licence*. If *before*, I'm sunk, in the sense that I won't be able to take it before next July and consequently I shall have to postpone taking the *licence* until November. If *afterwards*, I have time in hand and I'm safe. But, heavens above! I shall have to work. And I'm by no means taking on the role of idler. Tomorrow I'm going to buy the degree syllabus to find out. And when I get more exact information, I'll pass it on to you.

P.S. to this first part: the day before yesterday I began on geometry. I find it easy to understand, but I'm only on the first book. And then, am I going to remember it?

Friday, 18 August 1905

I'm ending this chapter with some information that arrived this morning. First, I've bought the degree-course syllabus. For the philosophy, they require only the *bachot lettres-philosophie*. I'm quite happy on that score. Furthermore, the preparation work for the philosophy degree is marvellous. It involves:

	Written	
French essay	—	Latin prose composition
Philosophy dissertation	—	Thesis on a subject chosen by the candidate.

Oral

Greek construe	—	Latin construe
French text explication	—	Oral test on philosophy
Oral examination on the thesis	—	An oral test on some subject taught at the Faculty and always chosen by the candidate.

Work of that kind is a dream. It seems to me to give one a chance to show one's intelligence.

The second piece of news is to do with Bernès, who has written an eight-page letter to my father urging him not to pack me off to the 'dump' again, and a four-page letter to me, strongly advising me to do music and philosophy but not to abandon literature altogether. Bernès is a very, very nice little chap.

You will realize that the effect of this, added to Mélinand's letter, has been almost to make my father capitulate, and I think he is going to agree to allow me to take my degree in philosophy. Now it's just the question of the bursary in Paris. I'm persuading my father to pull one or two political strings. But I'm nervous all the same; we've lost valuable time.

I've brought this chapter to a final conclusion and — as you see — on a note of hope and optimism.

✳

I'm going on to tell you about myself and give you a rapid run-down on what I'm doing at the moment, which amounts to what I am reading. Have I spoken to you about *La Domination*? I forget? My impression in brief: it's exquisite. But there's rather too much embroidery of well-turned sentences about nothing in particular. All the same, I'm being a bit hard since it is attractive and so charming to read.

In my last letter, I declared that Villiers de l'Isle-Adam was perhaps a genius. I think I over-stated it. I've been reading *Axël* with great interest. It is a fine and lofty conception. Nevertheless it seems to me that the merit lies in the style — violently tormented or superbly ironic and, at the same time, as someone has said, so musical as to be 'orchestral'. The weakness could be

113

precisely in too much straining after the harmonic effect which, in parts, seems ingenuously obvious. I'm anxious to re-read the *Contes cruels* to gain a more complete impression.

I've read Huysman's *En route*. It is, as you know, the story of his conversion. I admit to you that beforehand I found this conversion somewhat disturbing. It wouldn't surprise me if Paul Bourget turned Christian. It goes with his halo. Let Lemaître go to mass! I see no objection. His hopeless stupidity can put up with the stupidities of other people. It's already a bit steep for Brunetière to write *Sur les Chemins de la Croyance*; yet it's still understandable (though not all that easily when I come to think of it!).[5] But what knocked me flat was Huysmans. What the deuce was he going to do in that galley?

Now I understand, and I see the reasons that have led him to what he calls Christianity. His book is frank on this point. He begins with a chapter on the beauty of the Gregorian chant. Then he enthuses about Gothic Art. And you feel this is deeply sincere. Far from being no fool, he's a great artist.

Only, too much so. And it is art, and solely art which brought about his conversion. He was converted to the Christian art of the Middle Ages, not to Christianity. He is going into retreat in a Trappist monastery to decide the matter; the abbé advanced as an argument the purity of the offices they chant there. The first day he's on the point of leaving because he thinks the chapel ugly. What he favours in religious literature is the tormented, patient, elaborate beauty of the Mystics. He is so much a man of the Middle Ages, and his style, despite the influences of the moderns, is so naturally medieval, that he thinks and speaks as a man would have spoken in the year 1200. It's his natural habitat. Thus he understands religion in the way the citizens of the Middle Ages understood it. What he sees in it above all, is the Virgin, the Good Woman, the Devil and his dam. His tales about the temptations he undergoes are exquisite . . . and very ridiculous if you weren't aware of his efforts to maintain his seriousness.

Heaven forbid that I should ever want to make *crude* fun of the ingenuousness of Christianity. All the same, you have to be damned self-controlled not to burst out laughing when you read the story of Saint Simeon and his swine. It's a delightful tale provided you can laugh at it when their backs are turned.

114

I have a feeling that these accounts won't strike you as all that hilarious and I promise to reduce or suppress them in the future. I merely wanted to get my thoughts on Huysmans off my chest. Now it's done. And now all I want is to say a few words about Verhaeren whose third series of *Poems* I've just bought. It's stunning! What a man! These are the expressions which best sum up what I think and I've repeated them to myself at the end of each piece. No need to press the point since I'm going to quote. Guéniffey too is thrilled by *Les Forces tumultueuses* which, according to what I've read, are perhaps still finer. He has sent me this admirable poem [from the collection] entitled 'Vénus', which begins thus:

Vénus,
La joie est morte au jardin de ton corps.
Et les grands lys des bras et les glaïeuls des lèvres,
Et les raisins de fièvre et d'or,
Sur l'espalier géant que fut ton corps,
Sont morts.[6]

And further on:

Un Christ élève au ciel ses bras en croix
Miserere par les grands soirs et les grands bois![7]

Then this:

Le rythme de tes seins rythmait l'amour du monde.[8]

No need to press the point, as I was saying.

Concerning the *Mercure* question, this is how it is:

I kept the 1 August number for a long time, waiting for Chesneau to come and pick it up. He came here on the fifteenth but, using work as an excuse, didn't want it. So then I sent it off immediately to Guéniffey along with *L'Ermitage* which finally materialized.

There's an inquiry of some interest in the *Mercure* on tendencies in the plastic arts. It continues in the issue of 15 August which I've just finished and found fascinating. In *Nonoche* you will see the conclusion of the call of the *Tomcat*.[9] I like it. It's by Colette. The poems in both numbers seem pretty flat to me. Talent, but nothing original. Nothing as good as yours. I fail to understand your rejection — that is, if it's final — by *L'Ermitage*.

In the number of the aforesaid, I like Gide's sensitively chosen tones and their subtle melancholy. They leave behind glimpses of landscapes seen through the medium of a complicated but distinguished soul. How different from *Prométhée mal enchaîné*. The rest of the number is interesting, that's all you can say.

*

II. YOU. Although, as you can see from my letter, my brain's hardly functioning, I'm embarking on the second part.

First, a word to you on the question of 'posts', then on the hospitality of reviews, finally on your great plan.

1. POSTS. I consider you are *capable* of gaining admission into the Ecole *now*. I couldn't say it's certain, only possible. A year's work like mine this year and you could be in. It's not difficult. And truly, if I have failed, it's because I was well below form — in the written. I now realize that I was *capable* of being in the first five. You could be in the first 32 or 35 next year. In any event you can win a bursary and with an effort get the *licence* in a year. So, graduation in two years. It is already a qualification, and one which puts you in a favourable position — among the candidates in certain schools (the School of Political Sciences, for example). It's true that perhaps the diplomatic service doesn't appeal to you. Besides, I think you need money to get launched. If the Colonial service is your target, the degree will be very useful, according to what Guéniffey says. And then — it occurs to me — why don't you swot up for it next year with Guéniffey? Pairing like that you'll get through more work and keep in training. Think it over. I wonder if it wouldn't be the perfect solution. The Colonial service idea is a good one; it offers a fine opening for the enterprising and strong-minded. It doesn't need any further commendation. (Ignore my style. I'm played out.)

2. ON THE HOSPITALITY OF REVIEWS. I can't imagine how, if you wear down their patience, you won't bring them to heel in the end. They publish so much rubbish (see *Compère le Renard* in the *Mercure* of the 15th) that they must finally accept passable material. Wear down their patience. They'll give in.

3. ON YOUR GREAT PLAN. Frank confession: I don't like the novel. Of course you know what I mean and won't confront me with the 20 or 25 novels I love. It's the novel *form* that doesn't appeal to me, for three-quarters of the time I regard it as a bastard form since the novel consists of transposing subjective feelings, ideas, individual visions by grouping them differently, giving them a new meaning, attributing them to fictional characters who differ by definition from the original subject of these feelings, ideas and visions. That's why the novel so often gives me an impression of something overworked, re-arranged, pieced together. Madame de Noailles, using the novel as a pretext, parades herself rather too much in her books; I don't blame her, she's exquisite. But why then need the pretext which is nothing more or less than a conceited literary device? Why not confess openly — or make it quite clear that one is talking about oneself — as Laforgue does. For the arbitrary distortion he imposes on his myths makes it quite plain that it's himself he's relating, while masquerading under various names. All the characters in his *Moralités* are symbols of his ideas, beliefs, passions. They are exteriorized images. But who could fail to realize that they originate in the mind of Laforgue?

There is another way of escaping from the artifice of the novel to which I draw your attention. It is by creating a novel like those you put in your first category, a novel which is a complete, absolute world, totally independent, forming, as Bernès says, 'a self-sufficient whole'. The characters must live isolated from the rest and be what we stupidly call 'creations', and the world they see must be the world that — being as they are — they must inhabit. The trouble is that to write this sort of novel you require genius, since you have to *create*. The poet doesn't create. He echoes what he hears within himself and puts it into words. The true novelist invents, discovers something. The thing is, where does he find it? Since not in himself, it must be outside himself — in reality. He copies, interprets, generalizes by synthesizing his observations and selecting the most significant. In this way he creates types. His genius depends both on the acuity of his vision and his powers of synthesis. Yet, once he borrows something — however small — from reality, his art (in my opinion) deteriorates; for others it is a mark of superiority. In fact, I believe that creation after an external model, creation though it be, is not as good as the simple expression of the 'inner voices'. Hence my great affection for the poets and more limited admiration for the novel, even when perfect. And heaven knows how few perfect (even nearly perfect) novels there are. Among those I know I would cite *Don Quixote*, *Gil Blas* (only just) and I'd hesitate to look further.

Despite appearances, I believe that the contemporary novel does not exist. Or else that novels are concealed confessions or alternatively, strings of platitudes. The former can be fascinating, those of the second type are . . . legion.

You see that I am taking my lead from your categories in all this and that I reserve my hostility for the second — the Goncourts (whom I don't know, but am willing, following your example, to take as symbols). Furthermore, the vast majority of novels seem to me to fall into this second category. The other two embrace infinitely superior works, and, although I'm not mad about Laforgue for example, I prefer his *Moralités* to any ordinary novel. They are *straightforward* in form and, when all is said and done, do say something.

Now let's come to yourself. Not that I'm wanting to give you any advice, but maybe I can help by warning you against certain dangers. First, I admit that I don't really see any difference between Laforgue's conception and your own. I approve your idea of bringing your 'dreams' to life, but why do you want to introduce them into a 'novel', that is to say, give them a form which may let down readers that are unprepared for it? And if this is not your aim, there's no difference then — it seems to me — between you and Laforgue. This is not a reproach, but a preliminary observation — and unimportant — from someone who is somewhat in the dark.

I now come to a fault which I have long noticed in your work but did not want to mention because your recent poetry is entirely free from it. Unfortunately your admiration for certain writers shows that it has not altogether disappeared. As you are anxious to write a novel, I think I am doing you a service by drawing your attention to it. Perhaps I'm being cruel, but, thank God, we've passed beyond the exchange-of-compliments stage. After this terrible preamble, here it is: I think you have a tendency — though modified and limited by your other qualities — towards mawkishness. I've let out the unsparing term. I consider that you over-react to things that are not always worthwhile. Because I am afraid, for example, that your great admiration for *David Copperfield* and *Germinie Lacerteux* is partly the result of your fondness for sentimental details. The anecdote about the schoolmaster is charming, but — how shall I put it — a bit infantile. Such things would be heart-rending if they were true but in a book they are too touching. Similarly, in leafing through *Germinie*, I seemed to note instances of the same kind. And doubtless there's nothing finer than universal sympathy. Yet, all the same, you shouldn't get emotional about everything. Look, I'm going to be cruel to the bitter end; I'm afraid that in Francis Jammes — whose marvellous art carries everything before it — you see too many of these 'touching' scenes, created to move tender hearts. I don't find it shocking in him, but I fear you fall too much for that element in his work. So I'd like you to be on your guard. In spite of their indisputable talent or genius, Dickens, Goncourt, Daudet are perhaps rather dangerous models for you. And I'm telling you this precisely so you can avoid your novel becoming commonplace, as you seem to expect it to be. I don't mind if it's weird, affected, false, involved, as long as, for God's sake, it's not banal. Don't let there be too much to weep over; or, if there is, see that the tears well from a deep and genuine emotion.

Forgive, please please forgive this preliminary slating. I think it could be of use to you. Slate me too about anything you like — to get your own back. It'll do me good.

These reproaches do not apply moreover, to your chapter on Nançay, which is a perfect and delightful piece of evocation. And I note that it is precisely this fault of mawkishness that is noticeably absent in what you have written so far — it only comes out in your preferences. This is wholly as it should be. Thus I like Nançay, and I am grateful to you for having entrusted me with these recollections, and I beg you to resist any false modesty which might prevent your discussing such things with me.

I'm longing to hear what you have to say about the Tate Gallery.

It's not easy for me to promise you a regular correspondence. My time is not always my own, but I will reply to your letters within ten days or so of receiving them, without fail.

I am unable to copy out any Verhaeren or the Comtesse as I'd love to. I should miss the post.

I won't talk to you about *Pelléas* which I've come to understand better and better.[10]

And so I've nothing more to say about it.

What a host of things I've still to tell you, but, shaking you firmly by the hand I take my leave dear friend.

PS Until 30th — the same address. After that (the 1st) Chez M. Lafaurie.

1   Paul Landormy (1869–1943), musicologist and philosopher.
2   *Agrégation*: a competitive state examination, success in which offers admission to the higher teaching posts.
3   Author and musicologist. His literary masterpiece is the 'roman fleuve' *Jean-Christophe*, in ten volumes.
4   *bachot*: slang for 'baccalaureat'. The 'licence' is a university degree.
5   Ferdinand Brunetière (1849–1906), critic. The following phrase is Moliere's, 'Mais que diable allait-il faire dans cette galère?'.
6   'Joy is dead in the garden of your body. / And the tall lilies of your arms and the gladioli of your lips, / And the grapes of fever and gold, / On the giant espalier that was your body, / Are dead.'
7   'A Christ stretches his arms like a cross against the sky / Miserere in the dark nights and the vast woods!'
8   'The heaving of your breasts sets the love of the world in motion.'
9   The story 'Nonoche' (*Mercure* no. 195, 15 August 1905) belongs to Colette's early period of *Dialogue de bêtes*, published with a preface by Jammes.
10   *Pelléas et Mélisande* (1892), Maurice Maeterlinck's play, and the source of Debussy's opera of the same name (1902).

26   TO AUGUSTE FOURNIER

18 August 1905

I'm in receipt of a letter from you, which obliged me to spend one evening in the utmost parts of London. Thank you, all the same.

But, I shall be very *angry*, if I have not, before Sunday morning, any answer to all what I have sent you.

Yours heartily,
Henry

I'm sorry this p.card cannot give you an idea of all the gardens on the right hand, all the gardens and all the flowers around the palace.

H.F.

Written in English, on a postcard of Hampton Court.

20 August 1905   *London*

My dear Friend,

I've just emerged from a cold bath, after getting up this morning at nine o'clock, and I'm keeping my promise.

First, let me repeat how much pleasure you gave me by anticipating my wishes and including that piece by Verhaeren in your last letter. This and the surprise you gave me one Monday morning by producing a *Complete Poem* by Laforgue would win you a place in my heart even if I hadn't a thousand other reasons for being your friend.

It was so long since I'd read anything like it; I'm so deprived here of everything in that line that interests me that it seemed something more than marvellous, more than thrilling. I was deeply and delightfully moved.

What skill in *vers libre*, what handling of alexandrines! The most striking feature, I think, is the wonderful way he breaks up his alexandrines and returns to them after *vers libres* which are themselves marvels of dexterity and expressive power. Oh, those alexandrines which have *rimes riches*,[1] with those fragments of free phrases: 'C'était par ces soirs d'or de Flandre et de Zélande.' I think I still prefer this whole opening passage. The end is perhaps less original but yet so powerful, so compelling. What a man! What power!

It goes without saying that if you should have anything else so exciting and original . . .

Not to be compared, alas, not to be compared, but did you notice that in the piece of my own that I sent you certain *vers libres* were, like Verhaeren's, merely broken-up alexandrines? The major objection the Parnassiens and young Bernès had against *vers libres* was that the latter were always more or less fragmented alexandrines. A triumphant reply, it seems to me, would be to show them *vers libres* which are merely alexandrines transcribed in three lines instead of in one, and that single, simple alexandrine would never have conveyed, I quote myself unashamedly:

> *de vous être soudain*
> *mise*

122

sur mon chemin.[2]

What do you think of it?

I nursed a secret hope that you would send the 'original' to Rivière. I was expecting a card from you to tell me so. I would be very grateful if you would send it.

Thank you very much for your appreciative comments. I will argue about some of your expressions under the cloisters at Lakanal.

I think, my dear friend, that you are completely on the wrong track on the question of smiling. One can never reveal too much of oneself. You who love Maeterlinck know very well that one should never miss a chance of uttering some revealing word even if it is not destined to be understood, comprehended, for many years to come, and that words which conceal and smiles that lie must be regarded with horror.

The longer I live, the more I wonder too whether there are as many 'barbarians' as all that, or whether indeed there are any such people as 'uncultured' at all. 'O Guéniffey, O Barrès!' Every day I perceive that the sorrows I have suffered are the same as those experienced by others whose sole claim to be 'uncultured' is in their speech, manners, the way in which they express these sorrows of which they are perhaps conscious. There are no 'uncultured' people: there are only people who express themselves badly, others who have no idea how to express themselves, others who simply do not want to express themselves. There are even people who do not know themselves and that is why we must speak, when possible, in a way that reveals to themselves those who do not know themselves in order to help with their stammerings, arrest the flow of ugly words. Of course one holds these theories — far away from our teachers, Bazin and Chevallier; one ought to hold on to them even down there.

It is true that I am a trifle nostalgic at the moment, even for my Lycée. Any hope I have of not having to go back there is very remote just now. But you will still be there, and that means a great deal to me. My advice is that you should swot hard for the Normale; when you've missed admission by a mere two or three marks, you've a right to hope for the following year. I would be interested to know your score in detail. As for myself, I shall arrive with aims which I trust will go beyond mere aims. Here I am now with an encouraging lead in English; I noticed my progress in prose composition from the start; I can get along with French by hard work on the literature, in translation by swotting, in Philosophy by swotting, in History by writing to Meuriot the letter he asked for. I can get along above all now that 'my old sorrows of last year are over. My heart is free now, free.' There is only one person, very far away, recollections of whom can only give me confidence and courage, serenity and happiness.[3]

There was little else but my verse — or my prose — to interfere with my work. I wrote to Rivière, in reply to his clear, bold, disciplined plans, and pages on my own vague and hazy schemes. I don't want to say anything more about them from here until I've put something presentable together. All I can tell you is that following this said piece which I simply could not help writing and which I would have written wherever I was and felt simply impelled to write, I have done precious little. Only silly little jobs gnaw away at my brain and exhaust my body. I return home in the evening with my brain numb and lie down on my bed; and the cold baths in the morning revitalize my brain for the stupid little jobs that begin at 8 o'clock. All I can tell you is that I still have no idea whether the four or five pieces that I've managed to jot down are going to turn into poetry, prose or 'tales' or chapters of a novel, and that so far, I don't know whether there is one novel or several, prose pieces or verses lurking behind the mist of my projects.

And yet, as you had foreseen, everything, but everything comes back to me here, everything that is most profound, most distant comes back to me here, so vivid and meaningful — here where I have such sweet hankering after things past.

Only, even if it wasn't all 'prevented' by the factory, it would be interfered with by so many other things. It only needs the family — until I am completely liberated from them, materially, by some sort of 'allowance' — as you can well imagine — to oppose all my plans! I shall now have to undertake a whole campaign to prove to them that I'm not here for my amusement. They start by consenting and with expressions of affection that later become cruel second thoughts. At the beginning of the term I had a vague idea of entering the

Colonial School. I now see that even if my parents were in Paris, I should have to act in secret, for they will never consent until I end up with my 'admission' diploma actually in my hand. (All the same, I would very much like to have another look at the syllabus. Send it if it's not too much trouble and I'll let you have it back.) You can just imagine that when it's a question of poetry, what they'll expect for me is a seat in the Academy. Although it's a thankless task, I'm trying to prepare them for something different from the verses of André Theuriet.[4] I've sent them some Francis Jammes whose simplicity appeals to them. I've sent — using Guinle's music as the pretext — my *Ronde*. It was risky and I promised myself not to repeat the experiment. My mother replied: 'The *Ronde* is a very pretty round, as far as the words go, but the music — at first sight — seemed rather uninspired . . .' etc. (She reconsidered the music later, and my sister likes it very much.) I had of course appended a signature — other than mine — to the poem and so I was pleased with the appreciation. I had thought (and it seemed likely) that they would pay no more attention to those words than to those of any other song. But since then, it's all gone sour; the amusing thing is that they thought I'd got my eye on politics because of a section in my letters on the ideas — both revolutionary and traditional — of the English, intended for an anarchist friend of mine. In a general way, O Cavalié, one is misunderstood, misunderstood — one dies misunderstood — especially by one's family!

You will have noticed that I'm writing to you mostly about my 'inner' life, and not much about England. I think that I'll have all the time in the world later on to talk to you on the subject of England, that it isn't of pressing interest, whereas one's inner life is developing all the time and sometimes it's a good thing to fix it for those who are interested.

I merely want to tell you (for I've related it in detail to Rivière and to those at home) that I've had some exquisite walks through the gardens of Hampton Court (Henry VIII's Palace) where I went by boat, going up the Thames between banks covered with foliage, flowers, lined with mansions, houses like my 'Summer house'. The London suburbs (did I tell you?) are similarly filled with houses to dream of, nay, to weep over. At nightfall when the lamps are lit behind the small, diamond-paned windows and curtains like chapel curtains, behind the railings and the plants, when the pianos sound and the flutes join in — it could move you to tears.

An unforgettable walk again through the vast Rothschild gardens (by special permission). (I've described them in letters home and I can't in all decency tell you about them until later — 'in person'.)

Visited Westminster Abbey. Need to go back, since all I have is a derisory recollection of a pile of crumbling masonry which can scarcely manage to preserve the memory of a host of good fellows whom you forget, notwithstanding, sooner or later, so why not straightaway?

I need your advice before making a more intelligent visit to this and other historic buildings.

I've promised Rivière a piece about the Tate Gallery which he can show to you later. Two visits and I know the Tate Gallery from one end to the other. It's a very pleasant gallery, smaller than the Luxembourg, but when all is said and done, it is only the collection of Mr Tate, a generous benefactor.

Also paid a visit to Hampton Court, the Wallace Collection and the National Gallery.

Full of admiration (especially) for Turner and Constable . . . , then Watts, Madox Brown, Dante Gabriele Rossetti. Thrilled by a painting by Madox Brown.

Went to a comic opera, to a melodrama, and to a *music-hall* — same artistic standard.

All this at very infrequent intervals. My outward life shrinks daily. However, an incident last Thursday evening.

Can you imagine the sudden feelings of someone who, having decided to sleep and live for a fortnight in a house abandoned for two weeks by his hosts away on holiday, arrives one evening at six o'clock as usual, opens the carefully closed doors, takes his tea, and suddenly finds, on going upstairs in the silent house to his room on the second floor, that all the first-floor doors, all the doors which he left closed at noon, are wide open.

— Such were the feelings of your friend Henri Fournier at 7 o'clock last Thursday; not unlike those of Robinson Crusoe on encountering a human footprint or 'the sudden voice behind you in the desert' that Rivière talks about — as he moves up closer, sees the clothes from the drawers scattered all over the floor, the drawers flung on to the beds; similar spectacle on the second floor in the rooms of the two absent old ladies who board here — all the drawers the burglars didn't have time to put back, pulled out, all the little boxes, letters, buttons, rosaries strewn around — everything opened up, confusion everywhere, even in my chest-of-drawers from which there was nothing to take. I must confess, to my shame, that once I'd got a weapon in my hand, I was not a little amused to think that perhaps someone, taken by surprise at my arrival, was hiding somewhere in the place, then disappointed not to find him. Then, amused again at doing my bit of Sherlock Holmes (the descendant of the type created by Edgar Poe in *The Murders in the rue Morgue* and *The Gold-Bug*). So I did my little Sherlock Holmes act — although this classic burglary, carried out by professionals doing the rounds on all the empty houses in the district was nothing if not a routine affair. At any rate, I did my bit of Sherlock Holmes, noted the negligence of English policemen or 'detectives', made some interesting discoveries, invented some remarkable theories concerning a cigarette left on my table and the use of my gloves which I discovered in one of the downstair rooms. I shall be going through it all again with my host, hastily recalled and who has only thefts of jewellery to lament, whereas we still know nothing about the sums of money left behind by the old ladies which must be considerable.

I thought this little story would make you laugh. Tell me all about your 'outward and inner' life and your current reading.

Yours friend

Henri

Misfortune has robbed me of *Mélanges posthumes*, lost at (. . .)

1   The Alexandrine is an iambic line of six feet, which classically has a break after the sixth syllable. 'Rime riche': rhyming syllables in which accented vowels and the consonants before and after them sound identical, e.g. 'brûlante' and 'lent'.
2   The lines are from 'A travers les étés'.
3   Almost the same words he wrote to Yvonne de Quiévrecourt after their meeting: she was married by then, but it did not stop him from telling her she was the 'only one being in the world . . .' (see appendix IV).
4   André Theuriet (1833–1907), poet influenced by the *Parnassiens*, iden-

127

tifying himself with nature but in a quieter way than Leconte de Lisle, their leader. Fournier may be referring to his *Poésies* of 1896.

28 TO ALFRED BENOIST

[no date]

I hope you are enjoying your holidays, my dear Alfred, and I send you my best compliments with my kindest regards to your parents.

H. Fournier

Written in English, on a postcard of Regent Street.

29 TO MARIE AND AUGUSTE FOURNIER

22 August 1905

Thank you for the card. Thank you for the letter. Thank you. I'm waiting for Isabelle's letter. Much love.

Henri

Even this view [postcard of Marlborough Crescent, Gunnersbury] cannot convey any idea of the delightful suburbs of London.

27 August 1905

Tate Gallery

My dear Jacques,

It may seem odd, but I'm beginning with the Tate Gallery since I prefer to use my cerebral freshness for this chapter.

The Tate Gallery is over there on the other side of Westminster Abbey, down on the other bank of the Thames in a district of iron bridges, red-brick factories and chimneys.

The building stands alone, small, circular, ugly. The interior is like all English museums, spotlessly clean, disconcertingly polished. You're afraid of falling flat on the parquet; but there are chairs and benches everywhere so you can pause in front of the pictures.

One is not stunned, as in France, by the vast number of the pictures: there's only one row, at eye-level, on the walls of each room. It gives the gallery a cold look. It's a far cry from the dazzle of the Luxembourg. In the sculpture room, you have to seek out the pieces behind all the palm-trees. To be alone in the Watts room which is somewhat apart, is rather intimidating: but in a couple of visits you can get a pretty clear idea of the museum and it's very nice. I am going to try and give you this 'pretty clear idea' of my impressions. I shall follow more or less the order in which the paintings confronted me and also make my observations about the Gallery itself, as they occur to me.

✻

First, disappointment on discovering that it is nothing more than the collection of Mr Tate — yet rich and enriched enough to be a perfect representation of English art in 1900.

To start with, some examples of the genre that must please the English enormously because it is so very 'Dickens' (but there you are, there's not a single Englishman who doesn't know about him; he is thrust under everyone's nose on every side, and the factory is called 'Bleak House' . . .).[1] Thus, all so very Dickensian with its little old-world values, attracting by its humour, the delicacy of faded colours, scrupulous attention to detail, they might almost be transposed from Flemish interiors:

Wilkie with his *Blind Man's Buff.* When I think about the details, not quite naughty or saucy — a milder word is needed — I consider my Flemish transposition idea an interesting one. Wilkie is still interesting, if not so effective, in a dramatic vein, with his large painting, *John Knox preaching.* However, you can rediscover the same qualities though they don't suit the subject so well.[2]

Leslie. A whole *Sancho Panza* collection (I had already found quite a number in the Kensington Museum with illustrations of plays by Molière).[3]

Webster. A *Schools* series, degenerating somewhat into chromolithography. But only slightly, for if I were to mention to you all the 'Chromos' I've come across and that here as everywhere else, everybody's mad about . . .[4]

David Roberts. Interior of Burgos Cathedral. Quite small, but impressive with these same tonal qualities.[5]

I end this series in the way it ended up for me (after three or four hundred paintings which don't attract any attention) with *Maclise.*

Maclise was a close friend and Dickens's usual illustrator. This is a way of telling you that it all dates somewhat. But, nevertheless, I wanted to chat to you about it.

The *Play Scene* in *Hamlet.* Interesting particularly for his conception of Hamlet, a strong, muscular youth lolling on the folds of the Queen's robe — and for the remarkable skill of the composition.

A painting that begins to catch my attention — and which seems to me to mark a transition (with the former qualities still present —- but without the extreme minutiae of detail — and with an additional, somewhat strange and symbolic attraction and a technique — bordering on impressionism — in the colour harmony, especially in red and green).

William Walker. The Harbour of Refuge.[6] *Harbour* means Port. Red roofs, of a hospital perhaps, a green lawn with young and old sitting, exhausted, round a fountain in the middle — on the left, as underneath an arcade, an old lady offers her arm to a young woman — wonderful — blurred contour of the heads, impressive — low tones — weariness — the craving to find rest in the Harbour of Refuge. A little further on, *The Vagrants*, by the same artist, is disappointing.

I told you that these paintings marked a transition — but I'm not sure to what — the examples that follow show various tendencies. First you find men like Richmond, Dyce, the artist of *St John and Mary* . . . who probably qualify for the category known as Pre-Raphaelites.[7] The lines are too hard, the folds too stiff; colours either dull or violent lend to the whole the appearance of pastiches of Old Masters. Perhaps one ought to be more conscious of a modern, underlying sensibility and symbolism . . .

And now I come upon Dante Gabriel Rossetti, Burne-Jones etc. — a whole successful school of extraordinary interest but one in which I find two irritating tendencies that, although not displeasing in them, are repeated by all their disciples, imitators everywhere, by every commercial artist — two tendencies which seem to be distortions of the 'chromo' instinct: the tendency towards the symbolic and the 'chic'.

Moving on (I prefer to get this disparagement off my chest), you are confronted with handsome tigers leaping on to handsome partridges in beautiful jungles, but there seems to be no valid reason for entitling all this *Destiny* except that it sounds more chic.

And then the chic paintings, Art Nouveau . . . in profusion: there's the *Death of Chatterton*, by Henry Wallis, in a blue, moonlit garret, a death in a satin shirt and white hose — an *Ophelia* by Millais, skirt and flowers floating in the stream, redeemed, however, by a very Shakespearean peasant-girl head. A *Saint Eulalia* and a *Lady of Shalott* by Waterhouse which are really too exquisite for words.[8] Saint Eulalia, dead in the snow; doves fly down to peck at her, children and soldiers, exquisitely uniformed, arrive on the scene. The Lady of the Barque, white robe, flowing hair, in a boat adorned with candles set in the midst of water-lilies, the evening — too, too exquisite once again; finally, the *Ecce Ancilla Domini* by Rossetti, a maiden all in white. Evidently all this has its value, otherwise I wouldn't be discussing it all with you — but, a word of warning — it can descend to a very low standard, very low indeed; in a corner of the *Ecce Ancilla Domini* there is a kind of tall book with a lily on the cover — very, very artistic, so artistic as to resemble, line for line, the large pattern album of the Factory which is the first in Europe for art wallpapers!

I now hasten to add that the *Beata Beatrix* (*quomodo sedet, sola civitas*)[9] is very exciting, more exciting than the prints one sees of it — with the reddish reflections from the stained glass on sun-dial and hands, and, so exciting this head! — although it is very 'literary' and you would prefer not to rediscover these same, large cupid-bow lips in *Mrs William Morris* by this same, Dante Gabriel Rossetti.

Now of course there's Burne-Jones's *King Cophetua and the Beggar Maid*. Cold tones of the armour and the faces. Cold ecstasy of the king in front of the beggar maid. But I only came to like it on second thoughts.

*

And, quite apart, an unfussy work of modest dimensions which seems to me to knock out and surpass everything else and join hands with the enthusiasms of Père Franck over there in France and Germany, and take its place alongside the art of the XIV or XVth century: *Christ washing the feet of the disciples* [*Christ Washing Peter's Feet*] by Ford Madox Brown. Naturalism (to use Père Franck's term), the most profound psychology — so profound that Naturalism and Psychology meet in heaven knows what divine mystery. It's simple, sober, composed!

In the very centre, Jesus Christ washing the feet of Saint Peter. Jesus Christ, red-haired, straggly beard, tall, rather thin, absorbed in his task, completely absorbed and with a slight air of resignation. As for Saint Peter, he is wonderfully conceived. Old, white, bearded, corpulent, his legs crossed and his robe drawn half-way up his calf while Jesus wipes his foot — he is dumbfounded, his confusion is transformed into prayer, his head is bent so low that it pushes up his beard; he looks amazed and abashed, he is sunk in thought; and his hands on his crossed legs — crossed because of the posture he has had to assume — are crossed in prayer. This takes up virtually the whole canvas and yet all around, in the remaining part, is enacted the drama of the others who are in attendance. Some bald, others red-haired — bearded, with red noses. The man on the extreme left, next to Jesus, stooping down, undoes his sandal and watches — his nose shining. The one on the extreme right, behind Saint Peter, merely stares with all his being, his mouth gaping. And

132

from left to right the others look on — huddled, elbows apart on the table or with clasped hands. The whole thing is simple, free of melodrama and grandiloquent gesture — motionless. How fine it is!

I enclose this sketch of Saint Peter (the foot being washed is just off the picture). The eye is slightly exaggerated — I just wanted to give you an idea of the general shape.

The colours are reddish, hard, softening in the shadows, with an element of idealization.

After that, I landed among all the chic pictures I mentioned, then on to

Orchardson, with pretty scenes in a French 'salon' style — but the colours and details are reminiscent of the first category I described. There is *The First Cloud — Her Mother's Voice!* — words spoken by the father in a corner of the room, while the betrothed sings naively, and the fiancée turns the pages. Very nice. I note *Mason, Millais, Peter Graham* (I think on checking my notes, that *Her Mother's Voice* is by him),[10] *William Hunt* (landscapes) . . . *Goodwin*;[11] I noticed two of his very successful attempts at orientalism: *Sinbad the Sailor,* an enormous boulder, covered with seaweed and seawrack, painted in a sombre old-gold and, in a corner, quite small, Sinbad storing away objects which emit bright gold reflections. Further on, *Ali Baba and the Forty Thieves*: a procession in a flood of light, tropical flowers and colours, thieves on the way to the cave, likewise diminutive, in bright colours, looking weary in the vast, glowing fluorescence. It has something about it.

✻

Back to the XVIIIth century with John Hoppner,[12] then four breathtaking Turners. All four are in a similar vein and entitled respectively, *Aeneas relating his story to Dido, Mercury sent to admonish Aeneas, The Visit to the Tomb, The Departure of the Trojan Fleet,* and composed of large patches of dull white, faded red and yellow in which you vaguely descry an infinitude of luxurious vessels lying at anchor, processions of queens, towns composed of palaces . . . You don't see, you imagine. It is beyond my powers to give you any kind of commentary.

✻

Next, I pass through a central sculpture room in which there's nothing much to recall — on my way into an isolated room which has no exit, where I first notice a painting entitled *Time, Death and the Judgement* — three personages. My initial reaction to their symbols is 'Good heavens! This fellow is very much out-of-date'. Then, ready to damn the picture, I say to myself, 'A pity, it doesn't look worthless'. Then I realize it isn't worthless at all, and that the room is full of paintings by the same artist — his name is *Watts* (George Frederick). At first you are struck by his exaggerated love of symbol. That's all there is. Then you forgive him because he has sufficient strength and energy to measure up to it. With him you are always conscious of something behind, underneath it all. The sole criticism you can sometimes level at him would be on the grounds of his somewhat obvious symbolism: the globe, the orb, the sceptre . . . But he is an important artist.

And, heavens above! there are no two ways about it, you feel uneasy, a little intimidated, in this room. You're not carried away, you're not sufficiently calm for that. I'm dealing with all the paintings, one by one:

Time, Death and Judgement. Three huge figures floating in the void with the staves and some kind of Greek attributes. Enormous — and then, what one finds everywhere, a depth in the shadows, in the drapery . . . ; a kind of impasto or rather, merging of the luminous values, which brings out the figure in a strange way while leaving it in its atmosphere (I express myself very badly, but I have no clear ideas as to how the effect is produced).

The Dweller in the Innermost.

(Rain — storm — thunder overhead — which goes very well with the subject.)

A kind of nightmare personage, greenish, with rays — it's a bit modish, tapestry, Art Nouveau. However, there are types of bloodshot eyes with drooping lids which recur in

Jonah — marvellously brutal. Blind, lean, yellow, wrinkled, sanguineous — with the same greenish flesh tones, like those of a decomposed corpse.

The three *Eves* are marvels: *Eve Repentant, Eve Tempted, She shall be called Woman.* Each painting occupies a slice, a view of the enormous body which seems pulsating with life, power, delight, but sinks into consuming flowers or hides its shame in its hair, or glides over the sleek bodies of animals — tigers, crouching lions — towards the forbidden fruit.

The Minotaur and *The Mammon* are terrifying. The Minotaur, the red bull motionless before an impassive horizon, its hoof rests on a sparrow and crushes it. The symbol is permissible: there's more to it, all the same, than the bull and the sparrow. *The Mammon* is more interesting. Again, it's the terrible red God on a throne, surmounted by two small death-heads, crushing on its knees with its hand — placed there without seeming even to be aware of the fact — two little human beings, pale and naked, a man and a woman — exquisite, pitiable, frightening.

Hope. You know the engraving of the subject. At first (still Watts) I preferred it to the painting. But, on reflection, I prefer this purity of colour, the blue of the sky, the blue of hope. But symbols, everlasting symbols.

All the rest, I think, can be grouped under these four or five categories. I don't much care for:

The Court of Death.

The Spirit of Christianity hovering over the Churches. A landscape illuminated with the glow of light from churches: he wasn't meant for landscape painting. And the Spirit of Christianity hovering above . . . Good grief! All these pictures are enormous.

But I like *The Messenger* who brings the message to a sick man, a kind of desperate, resigned, meditating Jonah. It's the same as I've found with depictions of *Faith, Chaos, Space* . . . Always very problematic.

You find the personages from the *Mammon,* accompanied by vigorous but wild characters in:

Death crowning Innocence.

Love triumphant.

Love and Death — and, above all

Love and life. Love is personified by a swarthy, wild, vigorous youth. He leads a poor little girl by the hand to beyond a greyish rock. She is wonderful with her young girl's body, her childish head, lips too widely parted and two blue eyes, startled, yet trusting — very pretty.

All this with so much personality! Even before seeing from

135

the outside that the room had only one label, I was convinced that it was all by one hand.

However, outside I was disappointed to find *A Story by Boccaccio* by him which could equally well be a vast 'cartoon' by Raphael. *Dray Horses*, which could just as well be by Stevens, whom I shall have something to tell you about.

A *Psyche*, which he could have painted so much better.

Finally, I discovered a stray canvas in another room.

Life's Illusions. The usual childish symbols — you pass on — and find it very moving: knights charging at soap-bubbles — nude female figures in the foreground on floating draperies.

In a framed autograph close by, he declares that it is his best painting: *My best picture* (1902). If anyone should pass judgement on it, it should surely not be the artist. To me it seems less successful, less coherent than many of the other paintings, the colours not so well blended — also too laboured, the woman's figure, for example.

∗

I pass rapidly over the other artists who, compared with Watts, offered little interest:

I noted: *Davis, Corbet, Stokes, Rooke* and Biblical Pre-Raphaelitism; *Bramley, Hiltons*; . . . one or two attempts at impressionism which draw attention chiefly by patches of leaves and sunlight on the figures; *Hacker*; Robert Brough *Fantasia en Folie*.[13] An amazing female, but too elegant in a brown velvet dress with huge leg-of-mutton sleeves, toying with some strange, shiny, unnatural object.

And then Stevens, with a fresco: *Isaiah*.[14] Not easy to assess — it makes a powerful impression on me, but of overworked drawing. There's a whole host of skilful drawings by him all round . . .

Or perhaps there are none.

26 August

'Glimpse of self in a mirror — 26 August — finishing about three o'clock in the afternoon, on the second floor, 5 Brandenburgh Road, London-W. the 'Chanson de Route'.

———

I owe this appearance of a Mohican to an imminent headache which had forced me to tie this handkerchief round my skull.

Entrevision de moi, dans une glace — le **26 août 1905** — finissant vers 3 heures de l'après-midi, au 2e étage, 5 Brandenburgh Rd. London . W . la "Chanson de Route" —

Je bois cet aspect Mohican à un mal de tête lancinant qui m'avait forcé à me nouer un mouchoir autour du crâne.

26 août 1906 . 8.5.½

26 August 1905 — 3½ o'clock
    H.F.
    P.T.O.

I wrote these lines because I needed to work off my energy and very likely because I'd been reading Verhaeren.

I derived too much pleasure — unimaginable pleasure — in writing them and I dashed them off too quickly — two half-days — for the result to be any good.

I would like to dedicate it 'To the Town of Souèsmes — in Sologne'. But it would have given the impression of wanting to deny the influence of Verhaeren.

I eagerly await your opinion on these and the other poems.

Henri

1   Fournier is referring to the Sandersons' social club, called 'Bleak House' after the novel.

2   Sir David Wilkie (1785–1841): this was a sketch for a large painting. Fournier also refers to his *The Preaching of John Knox before the Lords of the Congregation, 10 June 1559.*

3   Charles Robert Leslie (1794–1859): *Sancho Panza in the Apartment of the Duchess*; and a sketch for the same painting.

4   Thomas Webster (1800–86): *Going to School* or *The Truant*; *A Dame's School.*

5   David Roberts (1796–1864): *The Cathedral at Burgos, North Transept.*

6   These paintings are by Frederick Walker (1840–75).

7   George Richmond (1809–96), pupil of Fuseli and influenced by Blake; his *Christ and the Woman of Samaria* is in the Tate. William Dyce (1806–64), like Ford Madox Brown, was influenced by the Nazarene movement of German religious art, and instrumental in spreading its ideas in England. The painting mentioned is his *St John leading the Blessed Virgin Mary from the Tomb.*

8   Henry Wallis (1830–1916); Sir John Everett Millais (1829–96); J.W. Waterhouse (1849–1917). *Destiny* in the preceding paragraph: there is no mention of a painting by this name in the Tate catalogue of 1905.

9   Fournier refers to Rossetti's painting of Dante's Beatrice in ecstasy, and quotes from the opening of the Lamentations of Jeremiah: 'How doth the city sit solitary that was full of people! [How is she become as a widow! She that was great among nations, and a princess among the provinces . . .]'.

10   Sir William Quiller Orchardson (1835–1910); George Heming Mason (1818–72); Peter Graham (1836–1921). The only painting by Graham in the Tate was *A Rainy Day*; Orchardson painted *Her Mother's Voice.*

11   William Holman Hunt (1827–1910); Albert Godwin (1845–1932) — *Shipwreck: Sinbad the Sailor storing his Raft.*

12   John Hoppner (1758?–1810), portrait painter.

13   H.W.B. Davis (1833–1914); M.R. Corbet (1850–1902); Adrian Stokes (1854–1935); Thomas Mathews Rooke — *The Story of Ruth* in three panels; Frank Bramley (1857–1915), painter of the popular *A Hopeless Dawn*; William Hilton (1786–1839); Arthur Hacker (1859–1919); Robert Brough (1872–1905), *Fantasie en Folie* — the lady is holding an enamelled jewel on a long chain and comparing its tints with those of a Chinese porcelain grotesque.

14   Alfred Stevens (1817–75): this oil on paper was a carton for the mosaic of Isaiah in St Paul's Cathedral.

27 August 1905

My dear Jacques,

You will find six large pages on the Tate Gallery which I spent the whole of this morning writing for you. The result will be to curtail this letter by the same amount.

You'll also find poems on which I spent the whole of yesterday afternoon. I had a sudden, mad impulse to interrupt all the prose and verse — especially the latter, in order to compose these in particular. As I said, I found an indescribable pleasure writing them. I kept on wanting to burst out laughing. They kept me in a high fever right into the evening. It must be Verhaeren or something of the sort that was responsible. It's up to you to tell me.

You must also tell me what you think of the poem that Guéniffey is supposed to have sent you, and to which I attach an entirely different kind of importance.

At long last, in reply to my very succinct and very English letter to *L'Ermitage*, I've got back my poems and the following reply:

> Sir, — There's nothing we find displeasing in your poems and some of them show great sensibility, but at present we are absolutely swamped with material and it would be almost impossible to satisfy, I mean, to publish you. At the moment we do not have an agent in London.
>
> Yours faithfully,
> Charles Verrier[1]

I detect not the slightest touch of irony in it, so I can write directly later on to Monsieur Charles Verrier to inquire whether he is still 'swamped'.

For the present, the lesson one has to learn is that there, as everywhere else, you need backing to get in. The 'swamped' conveys that.

A footnote on Charles Verrier's personality. He's retained one of the two twenty-five centime stamps I enclose — and he must have made an effort to say: 'There's nothing we find displeasing in your poems.'

At once I felt almost satisfied; it would perhaps be difficult for me to work next year with the beginnings of a work already in reviews.

And yet it is hard, I assure you, to say to oneself that there is perhaps at this moment a very blonde and perhaps very resolute person who is buying copies of *L'Ermitage* and the *Mercure*.

Of course there is Dumas who made me an indirect offer, but has Dumas any influence?

The other day, whilst reading poems in the *Mercure*, I found myself saying 'Good heavens, it's not possible that my *Grand Chemin gris* is rejected!' But what one needs is patrons, patrons!

What do you make of all this?

*

I'm passing straight on to your 'slating': just think that in opening your letter, my eyes lighted on it immediately and that I summoned up the courage to read it from start to finish before properly taking it all in.

It goes without saying that I readily accept criticism coming from you as readily as I accept your compliments. When you say to me: 'Your story of the little English girl was delightful', I'm really pleased. When you go for me, I look within to examine myself conscientiously. In both cases, my friendship remains constant. It must be so, and even if I *had* to give you the telling-off you invite, if I *had* any reproaches to make, it would be on the subject of criticisms you *don't* make!

That is all right in letters. But even so, I'm not sure whether in my letter about Nançay where I'm talking about 'good fellowship among sportsmen', you didn't think: Ah yes, Denis, Denis Diderot! I'm not sure that your liking for Nançay isn't to console me for the slating you gave me. But I reserve my reproaches more for your other criticisms, all those you haven't yet made, all those you refrain from making. In any event, you've made enormous strides under that heading, vigorous progress there as elsewhere. Your reproaches are therefore for the most part retrospective. But it has often upset me to see you pay a grudging compliment about items you didn't like by Guinle and about things of mine you didn't like either. You see, I consider that it's almost a way of letting down one's friends and you should at least have the courage to say: it's stupid when it is so, and the courage not to say: 'very chic'

141

when it's manifestly stupid and which the offender is bound to realize sooner or later and then lose some of the confidence he has in his friend.

So, your criticism has been a kind of comfort. And I'm all the keener to let you know, first, that in due course I'll state my defence. Yes, certainly. Be assured on this point, I'm not objecting to criticism, I object to its contents; my immediate reaction was to say to myself: 'Of course, I'm a sentimentalist! But then I can justify it.'

My second:

'All that's a matter of words. It's sentimentality when it doesn't come off; it's art, sorrow and life when it does. If, sir, you had read *Germinie Lacerteux*, instead of talking about it after a casual leafing through, you would have noticed that a whole chapter is devoted to Mère Jupillon: sentimentality of the slum personified as woman — and that the rest is indeed sorrow, life, art — it's Germinie. If you had read *David Copperfield*, you would have noticed that I had avoided indulging in fine writing myself apropos the assistant master episode and that I had narrated it in the most casual and simplistic way possible, thus demonstrating that I merely wanted to narrate it and was in no way trying to convey Dickens's art, its sobriety, its way of holding up the world at this story, and of keeping life going "at full steam . . ."

May I repeat it and add that Dickens, the great novelist and humorist, won me over by his sensibility, and especially by his astonishing skill. For example, the great humorist that he is, he repeated sayings, and phrases (another way of creating a world which is exclusively the world of his story) but with his alert mind, he soon realized how moving these repetitions could become — and his novels in their abundance of veritable leitmotivs, anticipate D'Annunzio.'

That was and continues to be my line of thought . . . namely that you've got it hopelessly wrong — or to be more precise, you haven't looked at it closely enough.

I've always preferred not to formulate, not to sum up unsatisfactorily what, given time, I could express more effectively, but you are forcing me to do so:

Well then, I've always had a horror of the classics, worship of the classical, phrases that are automatically repeated, poems which have no connection with life, which are on the side of Art when life is on the other, all the paraphernalia of the Muses, alexandrines and books, etc.

I've always wanted something which touches (in the sense of putting a hand on your shoulder), which pulls you up and stirs your imagination.

I've enjoyed Laforgue though you can't proceed without pausing now and then. I've enjoyed Francis Jammes because he hasn't divorced life from art, though I would have preferred him not to mention the fact. And the only minor distress that your criticism has caused me was the realization that I had been slightly wrong when I said to myself: 'We repeat these verses, we both admire, we make no comment but understand why we admire them — it is so obvious and we understand each other so well.' A disenchantment that I am now making an effort to overcome.

Of course, to gain the reader's attention, one will touch him anywhere; the surest spot and also the easiest to touch will be his heart. But then it can all become very feeble (like my images that hint at cerebral exhaustion!), very feeble — one can fail to be effective and, like you, I think it is always better to arrest the reader by other means than tears.

I think that sentimentality — going back to what I've said before — is always a false, hasty, over-facile solution. You did well to put me on my guard against it in the context of the novel, which, as prose, is less worked over, more sustained, quicker.

(In our discussions with Guéniffey concerning the 'artificiality' of the novel, we had said more or less what you have now set down so perfectly. I'm not going to talk to you about my own novel which is being transformed during its slow progress, transformed so much that it is turning into poetry. I'd have done better not to bring it up.)

A final word: my favourite piece in Francis Jammes is 'Silence' but I have many other favourites in which I am vainly searching those things 'to move good souls'. But Francis Jammes is not at all like that. When he says: 'C'est triste comme cette grille où les pavots pourrissent', one is not pulled up at all by the sadness. When he says: 'Que son uniforme lui allait!'[2] one is almost furious that the youth had to die at the age of sixteen for him to produce that phrase.

As for Laforgue, he buttonholes you at every street-corner. Sometimes he grabs at you, he laughs — and there it is — after all, it's better than unbridled sentimentality. And it comes off so well. It's so special, to quote the other chap. And he has so many resources, so many ways of arresting your attention, that you find he doesn't need tears, and forgive him when he invokes them. My favourite piece of his is 'La Connaissance en mai'. Have you got a copy for re-reading so that you can note the strange diversity of means he employs for evoking and engaging one's interest? Another piece I particularly like is: 'Le fleuve a son repos dominical'. I am truly sorry he had the girl throw herself into the river, but it seemed to me that this was quite clearly only a symbol of those lonely and desperate Sundays.

The fact remains that, like everyone else, I am a Mère Jupillon in trousers when I am below standard — and I must be particularly so in my correspondence when to convey an impression, I opt for the easiest and readiest solution.

The fact remains that I shall always avoid defining my position as much as possible, or writing to formula, and I believe only in a prolonged searching for words which will give the initial and final impression — and that I put all my faith in poetry.

✻

Now I am ashamed of what I'm about to do. Forgive me, I'm tired out. I must have been writing like a numbskull. By yesterday, I had exhausted my whole supply of grey matter.

Now, after talking exclusively about myself, it's where I'm going to end. Consider these letters as mere fragments of a whole which will never be complete. This time I've got through a little of the task. I'll get through the rest another time. I merely want to tell you straight away that Mélinand's letter was only as I expected.

— that I had thought of Landormy without even wanting to compare you to him — he has seemed to me something of a show-off.

— that I expected no less from young Bernès.

— that, way back some forty years ago, the candidates for

the *Agrégation de philo* were almost automatically accepted for the Science degree. I have it from our headmaster at Bourges, a former teacher of philosophy at Marseilles.

— that I would very much like to do Geometry and English with you.

— that Vigier, on his way through London to spend a month in England, passed a morning with me. And that he provided me with a yardstick to gauge the *enormous* progress I've made.

— that your reports interest me immensely and suggest bright ideas *about* books *about which* I was wanting to have suggestions.

— that I devoured the 1 August number of the *Mercure* sent to me by Guéniffey.

— that, with my present appetite, I've hardly bothered at all about the standard of the articles. I swallowed it all down. I'll discuss them with you along with those of 15 July, 15 August, etc . . . that I am waiting for.

— that I thank you very much for the encouragement you give me about the Ecole.

— and that *Pelléas* symbolizes for me at this moment everything in the world that is remote, French and friendly.

To you, symbolized not a little by *Pelléas*, I proffer an exhausted hand.

Henri

Your last letter cost me fivepence. Don't curtail the next ones because of that, but like me, use thin paper — even though I shall be obliged to pay fivepence postage due on this one!

I shall be glad to have everything, verse or prose, that you send, since I've nothing, absolutely nothing, to read. I have nothing to do but converse in English, to write and to go to bed.

Send me some Noailles, some Verhaeren . . . For once, I found Rachilde's article on the Comtesse very satisfying.[3] There must be a touch of jealousy on her part and mine, I mean that perhaps one is slightly shocked to see her so successful after so many, many, many others whose lofty and neglected genius she perhaps puts into sugar-coated pills. One can't help liking her all the same.

1   Charles Verrier was appointed editorial secretary of *l'Ermitage* in 1905;

the editorial board included André Gide and Rémy de Gourmont.

2 'It is sad like this iron gate where the poppies are rotting'; 'How well his uniform suited him!'.

3 Rachilde: pseudonym of Mme Alfred Valette (1860–1953), literary critic and co-founder with her husband of *Mercure de France*.

146

28 August 1905

My dear little sister,

Your brief letter was lovely — very far from being confused. You described it all in such gentle terms, if slightly drawn-out, but with real style! You have a special gift for quoting mama's sayings, so true to life; one seems to hear her speaking.

And I'd love to be there . . . But I'm not sure whether I can manage it before the end of September. And now, at the risk of offending certain people, I must announce my plans which I think are the only reasonable ones for the possible fortnight's holiday at the end of September.

In a word, I want to live in a fortnight the two months' vacation I've been deprived of and for which, for the last two long months, I've been sniffing like a caged tiger. I want to swallow cubic kilometres of country air, after swallowing so much stale and nauseous factory fumes; after bending over desks for two and a half months, being confined for two and a half months in a small room on the second floor where my large '2nd Prize-for-gymnastics' body can hardly move between the bed and the writing-table. I want to flex my muscles, enjoy more appetite than I do here, where they give me one sardine and two spoonfuls of jam to allay my pangs of hunger, and I want to eat whole rows of vegetables, drink pails of cow's milk. And I want it to go on and on like that — for two whole months. I don't want to waste a single hour, as one wastes them so often staying in the dining-room, yawning and not knowing what to do. I would like every hour of this fortnight's holiday — if I dare allow myself to take it — to be planned out in advance.

I want to tell you that you shall certainly have me entirely to yourself for three or four days. The rest of the time you shall have me mornings and evenings, but you can only have me during the day on condition that you are willing to trot around with me.

I don't think mama will take the opportunity to tease me about these plans, supposing I don't manage to carry them out.

I have far too many plans, having thought of nothing else for the last two months. I've turned them over and savoured them too long not to put them into practice. And then, you must understand that they are much, much more plans for my health — imperious, irresistible needs, than mere plans for my entertainment.

So, to begin with, I've ear-marked the first days for you, for anything you want to do: visiting, hours in the garden, walks in the woods, to your heart's content — all those walks mama describes as 'immense'. Walks with papa and Isabelle in the mornings when mama is busy, walks with Isabelle when papa is working.

As for the rest, one or two excursions like the one at Easter with papa and Monsieur and Madame Gauthier, stopping off to eat omelettes, cottage cheese and salad. Some excursions on foot of course, when everyone will be there.

Even an outing or two with the Gagnières' boy if that would afford *you* any pleasure. My hope would be that it should be as warm as it has been here some afternoons so that we would have to drink bowls of milk in out-of-the-way farms.

And finally, since ours is the country for getting up an appetite, the country of space and fresh air, for hunting and shooting in the fir-woods, and since Marie-Rose has given me a warm invitation to take you all on 15 July, and you must forgive unlettered, busy people, depressed by the failure of their son (put yourself in their place), their excusable silence, since it is the country where we eat voraciously and finally, since I have a crazy need to go there for five or six days — the real fresh-air cure: off then to Nançay — for five or six days at Nançay — on my own if you and mama prefer not to come; or alternatively and much better, with both of you who love it down there where everybody is decent and friendly.

Those then are my plans. I've still a lot more. I wanted to tell you them now, even though I'm not sure of being able to carry them out, so that, if I think it reasonable to treat myself to these holidays, there shall be no disappointment. And thinking it over, I'm convinced everyone will agree that I'm right.

It must all seem very selfish, but isn't that permissible for someone who has lived two and a half months entirely in his own company!

The main plan will be to eat and to walk!!

Eating — It becomes ridiculous here. They argue on these

lines: 'You'll only be having an egg and some fruit at midday; but you'll be having a plate of hot meat at six o'clock.' In other words: 'You shan't have anything to eat this morning because you'll be having a good meal this evening.' Sometimes, when it's a holiday, you go from five o'clock — tea-time — to nine the next morning with nothing but a cup of tea and a little stewed fruit in your stomach. And when you come down next morning, ravenous, they offer you a little bread and butter and a *cup* of white coffee! As for the main meal, after the morning hours of work in the factory, work which like all work leaves you drained and tired, I am as hungry at the end of the meal as at the start! When I leave the table here, I would be glad to have dinner at Uncle Florent's.

And here, I think, is the explanation. The rule in England is to have four little meals a day:

Breakfast in the morning at 8 o'clock.

Lunch at midday.

Tea at 6 o'clock.

Supper at half-past nine.

They bother less about each of these meals than we do about our two main meals in France; since, when one meal is neglected, they make up for it with the next which follows shortly afterwards.

Yes, but in busy households, or when the wives are either lazy or stingy, they cut out supper and you begin to starve to death.

And here, to crown it all, since my arrival they've been serving what they call a 'French' breakfast — not a meal, only a cup of coffee! Then, not to mince matters, it's slow starvation. It's no use my buying what I can, or eating the rolls you send, I never stop fuming inwardly. And I can't help, as you see, devoting a page to this question every time I write.

Walking. I've a damned good need of that too. For some time I've hardly been going out at all on Saturdays and Sundays. I've now got a sufficient idea of London and there's nothing much left that I can get to see for the price of a bus fare; moreover, everything's closed during the summer. I prefer to stay in and write to you and Rivière and Guéniffey and work, as I did all yesterday and Saturday evening. My brain was numb by the time I went to bed on Sunday evening; I'd worked at my History, read some English, translated some Virgil, written pages and pages to my friends about the museums and other impersonal things. I hadn't a thought left.

You'll understand that from now on I'm going to work at my English, nothing but English, intensively for a fortnight, in order to try and escape around the 16th. And here the leaves are beginning to look as though they want to fall. My holidays! My holidays!

And then I must store up my energy for the coming year which is nearly upon us. Rivière has written to me for the first time these last days about the chances I have of *getting into* the Ecole at the end of this coming *academic year*. As one who has been through it all and given it up, who failed to get in by four places, he knows better than anyone else the amount of work that has to be done and the chances one has. Up to the present he had always said to me 'in two years' time'. Now with my English, he says 'next year', with supporting testimonies and advice. It is all very encouraging.

He has received stunning replies from Monsieur Bernès and Monsieur Mélinand. He is undaunted, but cherishes no more illusions than I do.

Back at home, I'm very much afraid they cherish no illusions except those they have about mine!

*

One of my Lakanal friends passed through London on Thursday on his way to spend a month in a boarding-house somewhere in the south of England. I'd got leave to spend the morning with him, and for the first time, I was able to make a clear assessment of the progress I've made in English. This chap, whose English at the Lycée was reckoned to be on a par with mine, was totally incapable of understanding, of being understood and even of talking. I had to pilot him around everywhere. He was amazed, and regretted terribly not having landed an opportunity similar to mine when I told him how I'd had to manage to make myself understood in the matter of correspondence and among the staff . . .

But — another of those questions which are probably going to tip the scale in favour of my departure — once again I spent heavily that morning on *trains* and lunch. Everything costs a great deal when you are far away, so far far away.

The Nightingale family returned earlier than expected — for reasons I'll explain to you later. You will recall that I asked you for money because I was having to take meals at the club. However, I had been left with sufficient provisions to make my breakfasts and occasional teas. But I've used it all up, and, in the end, I've just had to pay, with the room, roughly the same price as for two normal weeks, after I'd had to pay for them first at the club — I who believed I was economizing! It's the lady of the house! However pleasant she tries to make herself, she is really disagreeable. 'Our big lass' has been staying in Lancashire for the last month, thus relieving me of the little job of elimination I mentioned to you.

And then there's the husband who makes up for everything. But I'd rather talk about him later.

For the moment, after three days' writing, I'm worn out and incapable of writing any more, however badly. I would just like to ask you to remind Monsieur and Madame Gauthier that the time is getting near to let them know that, once they've decided, I will be only too pleased to send them all the information they require without delay — including a list of phrases they will find indispensable when they disembark. They should arrive in London next Saturday morning if things are to fit in. I'll be free midday. I could also take the morning off. On Sunday I'm completely free and I've already put in a request for Monday morning — and afternoon if necessary — which they be pleased to grant me.

It only remains for me to thank you for your parcel, to express my concern on your being so badly off for music[1] and to advise you, to whom this letter is addressed and to whom all these questions of domestic economy can scarcely be of interest, to read the issues of the *Mercure* which you will find in my trunk. It is the most interesting review published in France at the present time, although perhaps rather serious, for you, a bit heavy from every point of view. The fact that they are only odd issues is owing to the fact that it is a group of friends who are buying them (1.25 frs per week) and sharing them out according to their tastes.

News about Papa has always interested me. Is he doing any photography? I'm sorry not to be there to lend him a hand.

151

Love to you all, especially, yourself. Write to me.

Henri

(Nothing pleases me more than to hear you are copying out my poets in your notebooks.)
(My 2nd Prize for Gymnastics, which Mama calls 'a volume', ought to be a medal.) What explanation have you given them about the Sanderson and Bernard connection?

1 Isabelle and her mother both played the piano; Fournier's interest is echoed in 'La Fête Etrange' of *Le Grand Meaulnes*, where 'a young lady, perhaps a girl, was softly playing old rounds or folk airs'.

33 TO MARIE AND AUGUSTE FOURNIER

2 & 4 September 1905   *London*

My dear Parents,
    I am still savouring your letter. It sent me to bed last night glowing with happiness.
    I'm afraid you will have already left for Nançay with Florent and the cousins and are going to leave me to go there all alone. I am delighted that you approve of my holiday plans, but, in the first place, I don't know whether I shall take any holidays and then, whether I should feel like it. It could be that I'll spend them reading and studying at the desk in the little classroom. Holidays are for doing what you want; you can't be tied to any programme. I just wanted to let you know about a possible programme.
    I won't write to you at length this Saturday evening. As well as a head emptied, as last Saturday, by my single, literary work a week, a head, tormented by neuralgic pains contracted these last days, makes me utterly unfitted for any, even epistolary, task.
    I have only to report that, although mama with her menu has inflicted a torture on me that I am ashamed to admit, my hosts appear to have noticed that I was starving and now stuff me with slices of bread and butter. It was wrong of me to speak

rather unkindly of them the other day. The entire household seems at last to have taken me to its heart. There have been evenings with me reading, them playing the flute and piano which I shan't easily forget. They have their own way of showing interest in you, in what you are doing, what you want to do in the places where you've spent time. This you appreciate all the more because everyday language has replaced business jargon. And Mr Nightingale reveals unforgettable little courtesies even in his business dealings.

As for Britain, the Great, the Old Country — or rather, this England that I've probably seen in a different light from others who have seen it before me — I am becoming aware, have become aware that I loved it — despite my dreary work and solitary little life — or perhaps just because of this solitude. I am fond of the language too; now that I know it better I am making some delightful discoveries. In all this I take a private, inner, hidden pleasure, like the life I have been living in this language and in this country.

And now that I am about to leave them, I ask myself — rather like an inconsolable André Gide visiting the desolate Algerian deserts: 'Am I going to want to come back?' Later on shall I not miss the little world I made for myself, which belonged to me alone and allowed me to review the past without regret — where I worked quietly for the future, when the great joys were garden strolls, flowers and museums.

Shouldn't I keep thinking of the Factory this winter — of those who work hard and continually and always to earn their place on the lawn in the evening? Won't I need to remember that to give me courage? And won't I miss all those cups of tea that keep one going?

And I'm glad to feel that I am going to love this Old England (especially when I'm back in France and it will represent something of my own even more), since now that I am going to try to become an English teacher, it is going, day by day, to enter more deeply into my life.

For the time being, this three months' life is drawing to a close. Since the work has tripled and quadrupled with what it was, I've nothing to do but translate letters — and be grateful to have had at my exclusive beck and call a youngster who runs my errands and has an unpleasant smell.

Yesterday Mr Nightingale told me that they had never regarded me as an employee, and, it is in fact true. All the same I have never been free of the niggling threat of being treated as such.

Yesterday morning, a stroll with Mr Nightingale and the Spaniard, Mr Couchi. In the evening, working alone in my room on the second floor. No two ways about it; these holidays have certainly been earned.

Tell me what Robert has been saying and what his father has been up to.

Although I willingly pay fivepence (10 sous) for a letter that is overweight, it makes me mad to have to pay threepence, fourpence (6 sous, 8 sous) every third or fourth day for three-line postcards. Could not young Gagnières, for example, send me his fortnightly greetings on the picture side, since on the address side they go to the trouble of printing that all foreign countries will refuse it?

I've also paid threepence to hear from Monsieur Gauthier that he was unable to keep his promise. I was doubly put out. I feel uneasy that he should be thinking about me so often during his stay in Paris.

— *Isabelle is a naughty girl*, and when I think of the silence of some and of others being laconic, after the good start I have made, I now close this letter of only moderate length.

Love to all,

Henri

Without omitting to thank you for the money-order for which I had to journey 15 kilometres and pay 11 pence.

Does Mama Berthe still know how to make potato cakes? (*Oh! what a shame! Isn't it a shame! Dreadful boy! You dreadful boy! Aren't you?*).

[postmarked] 6 September 1905

Thank you ever so much, deary, for the Japanese moonshine, and the view on Saint-Fiacre. It was just lovely and so kind of you. A thousand kisses.

from *Henri*

Written in English on a postcard of the staircase at the Bull Inn, Rochester. 'In Dickens Land' is written above the caption. He is alluding to two photographs, one of a full moon, the other a view of the Chemin de St Fiacre at La Chapelle, a favourite walk.

7 September 1905   *Arcachon*

My dear Henri,
   Successive changes of address have delayed me somewhat,
but here I am:
   The *Ermitage* business. Obviously one has need of patrons.
I believed the little reviews to be more ready to welcome real
merit than the more important ones. But *l'Ermitage* is hardly
starving to death. It only accepts 'names'.
   I think the essential thing would be to please some intelligent
type who would then give you a push. In my case, I'd thought
of submitting an article to Rémy de Gourmont. I would have
called it: 'The choice of an attitude', or 'The composition of an
attitude'. I made a start but abandoned it. I was aiming to
recount the hesitations of a young man concerning the attitude
to adopt in daily life, about the mask he should present to those
who are indifferent. This had led me to talk about Barrès and
his teaching. It was this part that I had written with no lack of
enthusiasm but which soon disgusted me and ended up in the
waste-paper basket. For this reason Rémy de Gourmont will
continue to be unaware of my name. But you who are anxious
to arrive at a result, however modest, without delay, ought to
try and win support among the intelligentsia who are in the
public eye. For that purpose the best thing, I think, would be a
very spirited but not too complacent letter, accompanied by
carefully selected examples of your poems.
   The recipient? That's up to you.

                              *

Your poem: I say *your* poem, for Guéniffey has not sent me the
other one. He told me you had forbidden him to because of the
bad impression his handwriting would give. I insisted all the
same, since I'm impatient and expect it to turn up at any
moment. Thus, I'll confine my remarks to the one you've sent
me.
   I like it well enough, but I would be deceiving you if I didn't
mention that I detect a glaring Verhaeren influence. The
arrangement of the lines, the stanza-form, the expressions, the
general tone — everything is Verhaeren, and it would be a

mistake to give the poem a misleading dedication. This said, there are many things that I like, especially from:

Nous avons préféré la DEROUTE
sans fin
des horizons et des routes
DES HORIZONS DEFAITS, QUI SE REFONT PLUS LOIN.[1]

I like:
Nous n' atteindrons jamais les villes de merveilles, etc . . .[2]
The end pleases me less.

Now, I think the serious fault is that it is really too different from you, from your own style. I don't recognize you in it, or hardly at all. And I don't consider it to be an original enough creation to justify such a sudden change of direction.

How I've been telling you off, my poor friend, for some time now. But you forgive me so nicely that I'm beginning to enjoy it!

Conclusion: I am eagerly awaiting your long piece that Guéniffey seemed to me so enthusiastic about — really I am.

*

Question of criticism generally:

You reproach me with something that has upset me, even though 'retrospective' — that is, with having passed 'grudging compliments on things that are manifestly stupid'. I admit to the crime, but I'll explain it. It bears out one of my theories, namely that 'nothing is more futile or wearisome than to undertake an impossible reform'. Of course, I am well aware that one hasn't the right to say a priori that a reform is not possible. All the same, I knew Guéniffey well enough to know that in saying to him 'this is idiotic', I would merely upset him and he would remain convinced that he had genius. I knew that because I had already attempted to make him jettison certain absurdities (his Nocturne on a theme of the Maladetta, for example) and you know with what success. As I also know that Guinle is incapable of discriminating where praise is concerned, I said to myself: Let us spare ourselves the pain of a pointless argument by eulogizing the good and the bad at one go.

As far as you are concerned, I have no recollection of having consciously acquiesced in these absurdities (that is to say, in things I might have deemed as such). If I have done so, it was from mere intellectual laziness. And I recognize that I am frequently guilty of these bouts of inertia during which the likelihood of an argument appears to me as the most frightful torment.

Question settled.

✳

The more specific question of mawkishness.

You are right: maudlin sentimentality doesn't come off. Nevertheless, all failure cannot be ascribed to sentimentality. It's a flaw in your particular mode of expression which is sentimental. The question can be summed up thus: watch your style, or there's a danger of your becoming maudlin.

I see that I'm being ruthless and going far beyond what I intended. Maudlin! No, you were never that, though it seemed to me that you had a tendency in that direction. Now, I simply cannot think why, and wonder whether my having suspected you of this weakness is not due to the fact that our temperaments are poles apart. Such could well be the case.

The rest of my observations amount to this: I believe I shall never really be able to enjoy either *Germinie Lacerteux*, *David Copperfield* or *Froment jeune et Risler aîné*.[3] They don't, I think, suit my temperament. And here I grasp the fundamental difference between us:

'We don't set the same value on irony.'

I can say (with reservations of course) that I never thoroughly enjoy a book that is totally devoid of irony. Not that I consider irony the supreme, ultimate element, the ineluctable conclusion of all profound observation. Perhaps in the very last resort it has to be sacrificed. But I give it a high priority in my normal way of looking at things. It is a quality I understand. It is not a question of superficial raillery, satire or humour. This irony can have charm. It can be and often is stupid when it is ingenuous.

I mean by *irony* the art of not believing too earnestly in one's convictions, of not having too much faith in things, of not taking anything too seriously. By this you will understand that

158

all unrestrained compassion that lacks a sound rational basis seems to me sentimentality in literature. My contempt arises from the fact that I've had my little crisis of sentimentality and universal pity. Would I otherwise have any right to this feeling?

It is only fair that I should admit to being under the influence of Barrés,[4] who is affecting my attitude in many ways and undermining any too strongly rooted conviction on my part. But if by nature I was not disposed to undergo this influence, would I succumb to it? Assuredly not.

The proof is — I hark back to my original theme — that Barrès has not influenced you. And why? Precisely because your temperament differs from mine in this respect.

Is it a cause for regret? I don't think so. And it would be betraying my scepticism to consider my attitude of mind as the only possible and legitimate one. The fanatic imagines an ideal universe made in his own image. Not I.

I wonder whether you understand how I've been side-tracked on to such considerations which seem outside the question of pure literature that we were discussing before. If you do, all is saved, and we both have benefited from this little difference of opinion which has enabled us to define our respective attitudes in more precise terms.

And so I return to the literary debate. And I say: I accept any sincere and successful work. Don't try — as I first urged you — to avoid sentimentality. Just try not to bungle it.

Francis Jammes. Admirable, because he is never unsuccessful — and also because he is endowed with that admirable gift of irony — and also for many other reasons — and above all because he is a great, a very great poet. But put him in the hands of a superficial reader. If the book appeals to him, you can be sure it is because he hasn't understood it and will have imagined sentimental passages that are not there (they are not there because Jammes doesn't believe too much in what he says and is careful to preserve his inward smile). That's what I meant.

Laforgue. I'm beginning to like him in retrospect (I don't possess any work by him). I like him for his irony. I would have liked him better if he didn't complain so much about his sorrows.

Henri de Régnier. I mention him because he likewise marks the parting of the ways of our respective temperaments. I like

159

him because he has chosen what is best in himself with such finesse and has shed every element of ingenuousness so scrupulously. He has selected from within himself with so much care that he soon ceased to find anything to say which seemed to him worth saying. And having reached that point he has been content to compose verse and write.

You don't care for Henri de Régnier (you take my meaning) because he has not stated everything that moved him, because he has betrayed nature by interpreting it (to select is to interpret). Your taste for Verhaeren derives from the fact that he has exercised a far less strict control of his emotions, has extended his interest to embrace practically everything, to the extent that he considers everything deserving of attention.

Would it not be absurd to ask ourselves which one of us is right?

*

What a rare delight to do 'ideology'! I can't imagine anything like it. But I must finish now, and that's really a bore! I want to make a rapid little encyclopedia of this final chapter, as you have done with yours.

1. I do not think — I haven't got it in front of me — that I admired 'Nançay' as a way of making up for my slating. It was truly evocative.

2. Thanks very much for the 'Tate Gallery'. It's a valuable document. From this point of view, England has helped you to make progress in — what shall I say — usefulness. You can be of service. You appear to be becoming more practical.

I believe the Pre-Raphaelites to be merely very gifted men-of-letters.

Watts must be something more, or so it would seem, judging by the reports in the *Mercure* (some critics value him highly).

Watts and Turner seem to me to sum up nineteenth century English painting.

Stevens is known. I've no idea what his standing is.

3. My reading. Just a word or two. First, Barrès, whom I read with undiluted pleasure. He is surely a great revelation and I still find it difficult to forsee the enormous influence he is going to have on me.

I have read the first trilogy, *Sous l'oeil des barbares, Un*

Homme libre, *Le Jardin de Bérénice*. I understand him too well to make any comment. I intended to include some quotations for you, but I soon realized it would be futile.

However, here is the concluding part of a chapter:

> Sometimes, in the cool of the evening, after those days in the Midi that are so heavy with sensuality, her mother, a distraught young woman, totally absorbed in grief for her old husband, would dress her up ready for going out. The setting sun sent its rays into the mirror of the wardrobe, strongly perfumed with Languedoc herbs, and her mother would bring out a little red velvet hat to put on her head. It filled the child with a deep sense of beauty, making her nerves tingle in a delightful ecstasy and sending shivers of exquisite agony through her being. But she managed to control her emotions until she reached the road where her mother drew to one side to exchange pleasantries with some youths. Then, in the falling darkness she began to sob, vaguely aware that the life of sensitive people is both sumptuous and sad.
>
> O, my dear Bérénice, how close you are to my heart . . .

I have read the whole of the *Triomphe de la vie*, if somewhat cursorily. I am very fond of *Jean de Noarrieu*, which is to some extent the development (though with less bitterness) of: *Il nettoie son fusil et couche avec sa bonne*.[5]

It contains passages of great poetry.

But decidedly, I am unable to bring myself to enjoy fully the second part, the longest, of the book which is entitled: *Existences*. Its extraordinary and sometimes overwhelming brutality seems to me rather too deliberate and, above all, too long drawn out. Hardly any pages of those winged and subtle reveries whose secret he seems to hold. Too much 'shit', 'scram', 'filthy syphilitic', 'swine', 'dirty pimp' and the rest of it.

Maybe it's the middle-class still in me that is protesting. Perhaps I was also in a bad mood that day!

(Allow me to tell you that from my window I catch a glimpse of a meridional sea, staggeringly blue against dark pine-trees and snow-dunes.)

I have also been reading Emerson and Wells. (What do they

think of them in England?) I'm reading Nietzsche (*Par delà le bien*) and *Les Rencontres de M. de Bréot*. Pleasant stuff. But how painful to see such a great poet producing such elaborate writing!

I think you've had the last word on Mme de Noailles: one likes her all the same! That's how it is. I'm keeping an article by Rémy de Gourmont on *La Domination* for you. It is a treasury of good sense.

4. If you don't mind, I won't send on the *Mercure* of 15 July as I haven't yet read it. The 1 September issue is on the way. I'm not enamoured of the poem by Verhaeren.

5. I'm terribly sorry to have cost you fivepence. It was thoughtless of me.

6. I'm putting the end of 'L'Eau coule' after Verhaeren's 'Novembre'.

7. I've accepted my bursary on condition that I can take it up in Paris. If they don't award it to me I expect my father will let me have a year at his expense.

Write to me as soon as possible since I was late with mine, c/o Monsieur Lafourie, Villa Velléda — Arcachon.

Jacques Rivière

---

1   'We have preferred rout / endlessly/ horizons and routes / destroyed horizons, which re-form themselves further on.'
2   'We shall never reach the cities of wonders . . .'.
3   *Froment jeune* (1874), novel by Alphonse Daudet, which has sometimes led to comparisons with Dickens.
4   Maurice Barrès (1862–1923), novelist and essayist, became active in politics and committed to a concept of nationalism based on loyalty to family, region and traditions. The trilogy later mentioned by Rivière (published in 1888, 1889, 1891) was written at an earlier stage of Barrès' *culte du moi*.
5   'He cleans his gun and sleeps with his maid.'

8 September 1905

My dear Jacques,
  This is not a reply to your letter — which hasn't yet arrived — but to ask you to do me a service, even several:
  I've made up my mind, by working harder at my English, to leave on the 16th in order to recuperate during some shooting expeditions in the Sologne. So I've only one more week left in which to form some idea about the theatres and concert halls which are beginning their season again.
  The principal concert hall, the Colonne Lamoureux of London — is [the] Queen's Hall. I went there last night; I shall go back tomorrow evening perhaps with Vigier, who is coming to spend the day in London; I shall certainly go back on Monday evening, the concert being entitled 'Wagner Night' and comprising the programme as follows:

1.	Huldigungsmarsch	Wagner
2.	A Faust Overture	Wagner
3.	a. Träume	Wagner
	b. 'In Questa Tomba'	Beethoven
4.	Prelude — *Lohengrin*	Wagner
5.	Prelude to Act III (*Die Meistersinger*)	Wagner
6.	'O Star of Eve' (*Tannhäuser*)	Wagner
7.	Introduction to Act III (*Tristan und Isolde*)	Wagner
	Cor anglais solo. Mr H. Stanislaus	
8.	Verwandlungsmusik (*Parsifal*)	Wagner
9.	(!) Overture — *Fra Diavolo*	Auber
10.	(!!) Ballet Music (*La Reine de Saba*)	Gounod

✻

A unique programme, as you can see.
  What I want to ask you is to help me not to lose 99% of it all for us both. I should therefore be delighted to have a letter from you on Monday morning especially devoted to Wagner in general and this programme in particular — in which you will have spilt out everything you know and above all, of how you place Wagner musically and personally.
  You realize that it will be a double pleasure for me to go

along and hear all that to some extent at least through your expert ear.

It has to be admitted, though, that I would not be going wholly uninformed, since there is a programme on sale that contains interesting, less literary but more technical commentaries than those provided at the Colonne. Furthermore, Henri Fournier is far from being the complete musical barbarian you might suppose!

All the same, there's no comparing the hundredth part I would get out of it with the proportion I would receive, fortified with your ear.

So I wait anxiously — by Monday please — even if I were to receive a letter from you today or tomorrow.

*

I will tell you more about last night's performance later. Talking to you in person, I will have more excuse to treat you to a 'literary' account, totally ignorant of technical terms as I am.

Here unfortunately, I've been interrupted. In point of fact, I am writing to you from the Factory, so now I've only time to tell you before this morning's arrival of foreign mail, that among other items, last night's programme included

Valse de Méphisto	Liszt
Concerto by	Rubinstein
Overture to Oberon	Weber
and the Overture to *Tannhäuser*	

This last omitted from the commentary. Admired like a brute.

Give me the approximate address of the Larose bookshop.

Had things to tell you about the poems I'm going to send to you before long — as I don't expect to be seeing you in Paris this October. Will write to you again shortly.

Kindest regards. Apologies for this end at the gallop.

Henri

Notes on Wagner

Wagner — creator of epic music.

I am going by hearsay, knowing only a tiny part of his work and that very badly.

German music existed before Wagner. His claim that he was its founder is therefore as unjustifiable as it is monstrous. If you leave Beethoven, who lived in Vienna (although born in Bonn) out of it, I mean if you quibble about his being German, there's still Handel, there's Haydn, there's Philip Emmanuel Bach, and above all, there's Johann Sebastian Bach whose work is a universe, more complete, if not finer than that created by Wagner.

Finally, there's Mozart, perhaps creator of what has been called *pure music.* That is to say, free of any dramatic, narrative, descriptive purpose, contenting himself with a spontaneous outburst. His music speaks solely to the heart. As I put it once to Guinle apropos one of his rondos, it is a candid and perpetual outpouring.

You can hardly deny merit to a composer when he's invented that. So German music existed before Wagner, and it was the most beautiful there was. (German music already existed in the Middle Ages and in the 16th century with Gregorius Aichinger for example. Luther's Chorales, also, are I think, not without merit.)

Dramatic music existed too. Nor am I talking about the early composers whom I don't know and who doubtless were not greatly concerned about dramatic *expression.* Nevertheless, I find this concern, already very evident, in the Gregorian chant. The phrase, halted neither by the rhythm nor the bar-line (that is to say, the way it has to cut up into fragments, into *propositions* — of equivalent length), since these impediments were not invented at that time — the phrase, free and spontaneous, follows (albeit somewhat haltingly) the sense, the contour of the liturgical text. It rises, swells into exaltations and falls into infinite depressions, or melts away in delicate sweetness as it follows the cadence of the verses.

But although we find a marked concern about dramatic

expression, we are not yet justified in speaking about dramatic music.

We must pass over the 16th century, the so-called period of classical polyphony, when musicians sought above all to involve themselves in harmonic devices, effects of consonance or dissonance, and were content to give the ensemble of their composition the shape that suits the text.

Dramatic music (I don't know Franck's opinion on the subject), is an Italian invention. Towards the end of the 16th century and the start of the 17th, there was a whole galaxy of composers who had the idea of providing musical accompaniments to mythological pastorals. We have above all, Peri, Caccini, Emilio di Cavalieri who wrote Daphnes, Eurydices, etc.

Then comes Monteverdi — the great, so great Monteverdi who, with his Orpheus, soars above all the rest of them. It is ancient drama, if not rediscovered, at least reanimated with genius. Choruses alternate with recitatives of deeply dramatic expression. In the second part of his life, for example in *L'Incoronazione di Poppaea*, he changed his style and anticipated the future 'Italian manner'.

But I must hurry on. Carissimi and many others in the Monteverdi circle continued the tradition. In France, Lulli.

In the 18th century, an Italian again, Pergolesi, with *La Serva padrona*, founded comic opera, a derivative branch, the success of which could have damaged true opera.

In France, on the other hand, Rameau used his genius to maintain lyrical tragedy.

Then came Glück, who began by cultivating Italian opera, which in the interval had fixed its form unalterably and, instead of developing expression, stuck to the *bel canto*. So Glück, in disgust, initiated a radical reform. And without being aware of it, returned to the Monteverdi ideal — realizing how to amplify the poetic phrase infinitely by enveloping it in a sonorous veil. He succeeded admirably and for the time being everything was saved, since his disciples, Sacchini, Salieri, with their weighty contribution, became pedantic. Dramatic music became terribly neglected or rather, misunderstood. They masked it with a grotesque laugh, made it into comic opera which soon turned into *opera buffa*.

Mozart, who (in his operas) flavoured his Germanism with not a little Italianism, remained an isolated figure.

It was not until we come to Weber, that is, to romanticism, that we discover a renaissance. Weber was rejected by the Germans and went to England to die of frustration.

Then Wagner appeared on the scene — and seeing himself so isolated, imagined himself infinitely great . . . There was of course, Mendelssohn (1809–1847), but he has nothing to do with the theatre. As for Schubert (1797–1828), many of his Lieder are admirable miniature dramas. But they remain Lieder. Beethoven is dead (1829).

Thus Wagner is alone, and it turns his head. He was born in Leipzig, 22 May 1813. I know nothing about his childhood. I know that he was insufferably proud, extremely ambitious, but very high-minded. He began with two Italian operas, *Das Liebesverbot* and *Die Feen* — which were never produced. *Rienzi*, little better, follows next. Those between 1835 and 1840.

In the meantime, he succumbs to the strong influence of romanticism.

He plans, still somewhat vaguely, to replace the uninspiring dessication of comic opera with a vast, lyrical drama, the elements (poetic and musical) of which are combined to form a unique harmony. He was the first composer (Glück had made no pronouncement on the subject) to consider that the text of the poem should be noble in order that the music should be noble, and to avoid the risks involved in collaborations, he began to write his own libretti — a habit to which he was to remain faithful to the end. (Berlioz changed his method several times.)

His first (serious) essay was *Der fliegende Holländer* (written in 1841, performed in 1843). There were still numerous lapses of taste in it; sometimes Deland's role is grotesque. But he was already working on an admirable overture in which he systematically employs the leitmotiv idea. Theme of the Dutchman.

The leitmotiv is a short phrase intended to symbolize either a personage and his character, or an idea, or an emotion (the theme of joy — errors; *errores* — wanderings).

I couldn't tell you whether the leitmotiv had been used

before. In any case, it was Wagner who realized its potential and made a compositional system of it.

After the *Dutchman* comes *Tannhäuser*. It is a strange legend from old Germany in which Venus is involved, but I have only a very vague idea of it. Likewise of the score, and I don't know what they'll be playing to you.

Wagner completely broke with tradition and began to employ chromaticism — one of his procedures — for example, in the final part of the overture.

After *Tannhäuser* (1848), *Lohengrin* (1850, I think). Once again a German legend, not any use my attempting to relate it now (it's a quarter to midnight) and anyway, it is well known.

Next, *Tristan* (1852), inspired by Wagner's infatuation with Mathilde Wesendonck and composed in Venice. The usual formula: 'The drama of love and death'.

Before 1860, *Die Meistersinger von Nürnberg*, a lyrical comedy. It was something new. Wagner appears to be restoring comic opera, but at the same time endowing it with vast breadth. Despite the subject (the rivalries and love affairs of craftsmen in the Middle Ages), I am unfamiliar with the Prelude to Act III.

Then comes the Tetralogy, that is, the four dramas which sum up the national German epic of the Nibelungen, i.e. the *Rheingold*, *Siegfried*, the *Walküre*, the *Götterdämmerung* (1860–1880).

Finally, *Parsifal* in 1882. It is religious drama *par excellence*.

But, as I can't mention everything, I'll add a word on each item of the programme.

1. *Huldingungsmarsch*. I think it is Lohengrin's wedding-march — or the prelude to Act III. Nothing could be simpler to understand. It consists of a phrase which rises superbly and convulsively like an uneasy triumph (we know that if Elsa asks Lohengrin who he is, he will be forced to leave her).

2. *Overture to Faust*. I don't know it.

3. *Träume*. Study for *Tristan and Isolde*. It is noble, with inward strength and impassioned reverie.

4. *In questa tomba* (Beethoven). Attractive air of dignified sadness and very pure.

5. *Prelude to Lohengrin*. <> This is the sign Berlioz uses to symbolize this overture which expands like a soul, and after a

moment of sublime expansion, gently subsides. It is supposed to symbolize Titurel descending from Heaven to bear the Holy Grail to — I can't recall whom — and mounting up again. I don't know if Wagner thought of that idea.

6. *Prelude to Act III of Die Meistersinger.* I don't know it. The note of the drama is passion mixed with good-natured comedy but with its scope extended and enlarged by genius.

6a. *Tannhäuser.* I don't know anything about 'O Star of Eve.'

7. *Introduction to Act III* is the death of Isolde. The cor anglais represents the song of a shepherd, admirably broken-hearted.

8. *Verwandlungsmusik.* I suppose it is what we call the Enchantment of Good Friday, that is to say, the miracle of a valley suddenly bursting into blossom. In the harmonic fabric, so taut and so rich, we feel the progressive and marvellous blossoming-forth — the birth of vital energy.

As for the rest . . .

So, Wagner — epic genius. His contribution is his invention of sonorous atmosphere — he was the first to consider the melodic phrase insufficient to give the text its maximum expansion, and he enveloped this initial envelope in an infinitely profound harmony, the lowest registers of which go deeper than the soul itself. To such a point that the echo of the least significant verses is prolonged into hitherto unplumbed depths.

My overall impression: It is overwhelming.

Forgive me this prospectus penned in such an indecorous style.

Your *Jacques Rivière*

Reply to my letter and send me your new address.

[9 September 1905]

My dear Parents,
I will let you know the exact date as soon as I hear from Jean. If he's in Paris, leaving London on Saturday evening, arriving in Paris next morning, I'll spend the day with him and Monsieur and Madame Bernard and set out for La Chapelle in the evening.

I've had an understanding with them too long for me to break my promise at the last minute.

If he's not in Paris, I'll merely greet Monsieur and Madame Bernard on the way from the Gare Saint-Lazare to the Gare d'Orleans.

In any event, I am leaving from Victoria on Saturday at 10 o'clock in the evening.

Although exhausted, I wanted to pass on the good news tonight.

Vigier, my friend from Lakanal, to whom I wrote the day before yesterday saying that I would be leaving on Saturday, insisted on spending this last Saturday in London with me.

From seven this morning until seven this evening, I've had to take him around from one museum to the next in this vast city. In driving rain and at considerable cost to both my purse and my legs. We've had to take buses, walk, take more buses, walk again, visit museums, have lunch. But he is one of those I'm going to spend the coming year with and I've had a foretaste of it all day in his conversation.

Yesterday, at the same time as he gave me permission for today, Mr Nightingale remitted to me the little envelope that I enclose with this letter. Isn't it delightful to see me given a rise like this — to see me earning £2.8 a month — whereas when I arrived, not knowing the first thing about business and, despite all my previous education, having been, like a good many *bacheliers* quite useless!

They talk about using my business letters as models. Although I have always been so reserved with everybody, they talk about the excellent impression I shall leave behind. (And even then, it is out of modesty that I say 'they talk' — in point of fact, Mr Nightingale has asked the office girls to use my translations, from now on, as models for commercial correspondence.)

When she came in this evening, Mrs Nightingale had some milk heated for me and got me to try on all her husband's hats — in the drawing-room — going into raptures over how well they suited me.

Before I leave, or on my arrival home, do you think I ought to give the baby a present? I should like to for my own satisfaction as a way of showing Mr Nightingale my eternal gratitude — and also of leaving behind a corner of London well disposed towards me against my eventual return at the expense of the Ecole Normale, the year before the Agrégation.

But I await your advice; you can judge better than me, although you have never tried to put yourselves in my place, to see in what conditions I might have lived and in what conditions I have actually lived.

I have to add too that you don't take enough notice of the hints and reservations in my letters. When, for example, I say: 'It could be that . . .', you shouldn't reply as if I had said: 'I'm bent on . . .'.

But an end to reproaches. It's just as well since (for the last time), I have to ask you for the fare home: 35 francs and some small change payable, for the love of God, at *Chiswick* (London).

Weary but content, I embrace you in advance. Thank you, papa, for your letter. Thank you, mama, for yours. Thanks once more to Isabelle for her paintings.

All my love.

Henri

I shall arrive Sunday evening, 17 September or Monday morning, the 18th.

13 September 1905   *Gunnersbury*

(Up to Saturday evening.
Sunday: in Paris
After that: La Chapelle d'Angillon and Nançay)

My dear Jacques,

This is not a reply to your letter which I'll *try* to answer during the holidays. Although you've dealt admirably with some things, there are others which call for a reply despite my distaste for finalizing any view of mine on the world of art and life.

I just want to thank you for your Wagner prospectus and to say a word or two about some ten questions which I propose to expand on later.

I sail for France at 11 o'clock on Saturday evening. One of the reasons for the brevity of this letter is that I am anxious to *utilize* my remaining four days in the best possible way. Tonight I'm going to see *Hamlet* acted by a company that devotes itself exclusively to Shakespeare and is reputed to be first-class.[1] I am going to try and finish *The Adventures of Tom Sawyer* (a child, not a detective!) by Mark Twain which I began last night. It gives me an inordinate pleasure which I cannot, alas, share with you, since it depends on my near-perfect knowledge of incommunicable colloquial English. I had to be content with two chapters only of Wells's *Anticipations* since the book was due back at the library. And all my time was taken up elsewhere. I was expecting an 'after Mélinand' atmosphere, and found instead merely practical considerations to do with the present state of things — completely irrelevant in view of the potential revolution in the field of inventions and unforeseen discoveries (radium and so on). I still have to find out what this author's novels are like. Read *Oliver Twist* by Dickens and bought a copy. Read *A Tale of Two Cities* by the same author — a great humorist and a genius as a writer of serials.

Had decided to know what stuff Jean-Arthur Rimbaud was made of and buy works of his on my way through Paris, as well as *Les Moralités légendaires*[2] and *Le Deuil des primevères*. I found the Rimbaud in a bookshop on Saturday and had no sooner leafed through it than I decided not to stay a moment longer in such distasteful company. The bookseller made no bones about taking it back, but in the meantime I had read through and copied out bits and overcome my repugnance. There's undoubtedly something about *Une Saison en enfer* and *Les Illuminations*. I'll try and tell you what — perhaps it's all nothing more than a collection of epigraphs. At all events they came along at the right moment, together with the *Juvenalia* — Coppée gone wrong — which he later repudiated and in which he pisses *avec l'assentiment des grands héliotropes*.[3]

He came at the right time. I smile when I hear people referring to him as 'an incomplete genius'. All the same, he has been useful to me as a foil for my unreserved admiration for Laforgue. I now regard my initial distaste as very puerile and akin to the perversity of the book and one's other dislikes. I almost regret having had to return it.

I'll explain to you at greater length what I think of the book and how the strange idea of wanting to buy it occurred to me.

I'm replacing it with *Les Campagnes hallucinées* and *Les Villes tentaculaires* in the order I'm sending off to Larose this evening. — though I'm not sure of his address. I've long hesitated between the latter and *Phocas le jardinier*.[4]

But it seems to me that the best method of freeing oneself from the urge to pastiche someone you know is to explore him in depth. In this way you realize that there is something more to be discovered.

From this point of view, the worst thing is knowing just three pieces, as I do of Verhaeren.

Hence the unashamed pastiche as you called it.

Only, as usual I was wrong to have posted it off immediately, without allowing myself time to assess its worth and situate it properly, for I don't think it marks a step in my development towards *vers libre*. I was unable to anticipate the pieces that follow and which already show a break from Verhaeren: you should have left *Les Conquérants* with the rest and waited; you would have had a better understanding of this incomprehensible swing of the tiller if, in the light of the other pieces, you had been in a position to judge the new direction. It happens to be one of the few pieces of my own that I care about. It's always the same; you have an enthusiasm for a poet and a poor opinion of your own work when you produce an indifferent pastiche of the poet in question. That is why one is so badly placed to pass judgement on one's own work.

And so I am forwarding only the piece I wrote last July. It doesn't matter if Guéniffey has forestalled me. It annoys me to realize it was promised so far back. However, I've scarcely any liking for it left now, except as a document. Furthermore I don't think it corresponds in any way to what I observed and felt at the time. Always the same: other pieces on the stocks will explain and complete it. Now no alternative than to launch a complete book, and, until then, keep my mouth shut.

In any case I have little that's worth showing, no time! I will wait until I see you on Sundays in Paris.[5] For, heavens above! without seeming to, that's really what you were saying to me, isn't it? You'll be coming to Paris *for certain*, won't you?

I spent the whole of Saturday with Vigier. He really is too nice a little fellow. He was ecstatic about all the things I hoped he would be (with some pretty shrewd observations) — except regarding the Fox Browns [Ford Madox Brown?]. Have found a second-hand copy of *La Nouvelle Espérance* by Madame de Noailles that I leafed through.

On Saturday, four hours before my departure, I am seeing the English girl I've been corresponding with for the last two years. She is passing through London and is spending a couple of hours there on her way to Cambridge. I feel I know her and am waiting, fascinated, for my suppositions to be confirmed by the first glance that tells you everything once and for all. Fascinated just by the anticipation of the experience.

She has sent me a slim volume of verse written by one of her friends, printed for private circulation. It is how Francis Jammes began. I'll tell you more about it and about my initial antipathy to English poetry.

I am bringing back from this Old England with its exquisite countryside a mood of complete confidence and serenity and resolute and serene views about the path to pursue in this unreal world. My only fear is that it may all fall apart in Paris this winter. No, I have ceased to harbour this fear because yesterday I felt regretful not to have any sorrow to bear, any sorrow to conceal on these cold, grey mornings and in these evening fogs which have begun in London for the winter. No, somehow if I had any to bear, I would prefer it to be in this vast, grim city under these winter fogs.

And I am not writing to anyone. Sometimes, for certain reasons, I thought about Camille Mauclair.[6] But all things considered, I owe it to my parents, my promises and my life not to embark on this school year while waiting for a reply from that quarter. What is more, — for I would not sacrifice it for nothing, one owes it, as Laforgue puts it, to one's art.

I have decided to pass a year — not in silence — but without writing. To have a year or two of work and life free from all literary pretention — a year or two's serious study of the classics, that is, of one's predecessors . . .

Then, with some kind of post, that is to say a means of livelihood, so that I can live a life — not one but a thousand lives — recollected, imagined, expressed in free rhythms.

For I am certain of being able to emerge from the test I am endeavouring to describe with the hope of having something to say.

The sad part of all this is that twenty years will have passed by without my having said anything; and, at times, the mere thought of this makes me feel bad. However, whoever says that it isn't the ideal age to make a start?

The sad part, all the same, is that something will have to be sacrificed. I am frightened lest all this fades out, hopelessly, with the summer. And yet I feel confident. When the will is there, you can hope for anything, and I prefer to keep hoping and to stick it out rather than sacrifice everything to the vanity of appearing in *L'Ermitage*, to the childish desire of not being considered something of an imposter — childish, since, as people will discover later, that is what I certainly have not been.

All this scribbling I'm doing to you from the Factory is not properly composed and scarcely thought out. I'll come back to it all and especially to Wagner. Although I felt unwell and on edge, I followed the concert for the most part. I understood the overture to *Tannhäuser* more from the music point of view, being absolutely ignorant of the story. One feels a great admiration for the literary idea of a song which is sad for the *sole reason that it is so* — hence my admiration for the indescribably moving sound of the horn blown by Tristan's shepherd. I was able to follow all the rest. 'Epic music' — just

175

as I had imagined. I am all agog for further performances.

I am afraid I shall have forgotten it all when on some rainy day at La Chapelle or Nançay, I start on a letter specially devoted to Wagner, Barrès, Gourmont, Rimbaud, Laforgue, YOU and ME.

I have heaps to tell you about Laforgue. I am piously sending you one of my favourite pieces of his which please be careful not to lose. I've a great deal to say about him. I'd like to know whether Mauclair has left me any tiny thing to add. I am convinced that his irony is not at all the kind you favour. That's just another pin-prick, a further sadness. One should watch out to see whether, at times, it doesn't come under the heading of the sceptic's irony you mention. But I don't think so. Yet, what a wealth of poetry, of refinement, what a wealth in the simple 'Convalescence en Mai'. I will tell you why: first and foremost, your liking for Gourmont and Barrès has shaken old convictions of mine that go back two or three years — literary and philosophical convictions, of course.

I am enclosing a very early piece of mine which I *adore*! I find it amusing to see that I sent you the commentary on it two months ago.

Words fail me to excuse the ghastly style of this letter, written any old how and at one go.

By way of expressing my thanks for many things, I am going to send you, before I leave London, something that cost sixpence and will please you enormously.

Yours

Henri

P.S. Although You're expecting another letter from me, write to me all the same.

Henri

---

1 Perhaps the company directed by Ben Greet. The experience was not lost on Fournier: see *Le Grand Meaulnes* I:12.
2 *Moralités légendaires* (1887) by Jules Laforgue.
3 '. . . with the consent of the tall heliotropes'.
4 All collections of poems by Verhaeren.
5 See appendix I.
6 Mauclair (1872–1936), one of the 'Vers-libristes' group, dominated by Verhaeren.

l'art — deux tendances qui ne me paraissent que des déformations de l'instinct "chromo" : la tendance au Symbole, et au Chic.

On va trouver (plus loin, mais je préfère en finir tout de suite avec cet éreintement) de beaux tigres qui sautent sur de belles perdrix dans de belles jungles, mais il n'y a pas de raison d'intituler ça "le Dessin" — sinon que c'est plus chic.

Et alors des tableaux chic, art nouveau — à profusion : c'est "Une mort de Chatterton" par Henry Wallis, dans une mansarde bleue de lune, une mort en habit de soie et en bas blancs — une "Ophélia" de Millais, jupe et fleurs flottantes au courant qui se rachète pourtant par une tête paysanne bien Shakespearienne — une "Sainte Eulalie" et une "Lady of the Shalott" de Waterhouse qui sont trop trop exquises. La Sainte Eulalie morte dans la neige, des colombes viennent la becqueter et des enfants et des soldats en costumes exquis arrivent. La Dame de la Barque, robe blanche et cheveux tombants, dans une barque garnie de cierges, au milieu des nymphéas, le soir — trop exquis, trop exquis. trop exquis encore, enfin, même le "Ecce Ancilla Domini" de Rossetti, une jeune fille toute blanche ; même "l'Annunciation" de Rossetti une jeune fille et un jeune ange tout blancs. Maintenant, évidemment, tout cela a sa valeur, sans quoi je ne t'en parlerais pas, seulement il faut se méfier, ça peut tomber bas, bas ; il y a dans le coin de "Ecce Ancilla Domini" une espèce d'album de forme longue avec un lis sur la couverture, très très artistique, si artistique qu'il ressemblerait pour trait aux grands albums d'échantillons de la Factory qui est la première d'Europe pour les papiers peints Artistiques !

—— Maintenant, j'ai hâte de dire que la "Beata Beatrix" (Quomodo Sedet, sola Civitas) est très emballante, plus emballante que les gravures qu'on a vu autrefois avec des reflets rougeâtres de vitraux sur le cadran solaire et sur les mains. Et si emballante, cette tête ! — encore que ce soit beaucoup de la Littérature, encore qu'on préférerait ne pas retrouver ces grandes lèvres formulées chez "Mrs William Morris" du même Dante Gabriele Rossetti.

Maintenant, évidemment, il y a Burne Jones "King Cophetua and the Beggar Maid" Tons froids des cuirasses et des visages. Extase froide du roi devant la Mendiante. Mais je crois ne pas l'avoir aimé que à la réflexion.

             ×

Et tout à côté il y a une œuvre sans tapages, de dimensions moyennes, qui me paraît bien riche tout par terre et par ses pas besoin, tout pour donner la main aux enthousiasmes, du père Franck, par la fin, en France et en Allemagne, du côté du 14e ou du XVe —

"Le Christ lavant les pieds de Apôtres" par Ford Madox Brown

20 September 1905   *Arcachon*
& following days

My dear Henri,

As I am beginning to get a bit bored here, I'm writing to you. I mention this so that you won't feel fed up with me for writing so often.

First, thank you very much for the parcel. You will realize that I was very touched: the intention was marvellous, the article itself no less. And the great merit of this little book is that it is a document. So please accept my gratitude.

As a reward, I'm going to serve up a brief commentary on your poem.[1]

General impression: it is good and, at times, very good.

General criticism: it is rather vague — how shall I put it — in its tendency. The influence of Francis Jammes is undeniable, and yet it is not Francis Jammes. This — which may appear to be a eulogy — will be explained (literally) when I come to a detailed analysis. One other general observation: the *vers libre* (handled, I must say, with great skill) is a little disconcerting; since Jammes' verse, as someone said, is 'freed' but not 'free' verse. Thus these very Jammes-like and charming touches seem somewhat strange in this form. This, I think, lies behind the indecisiveness which emerges, despite everything, as the final impression.

Detailed criticism: the dedication is very nice. Indeed, 'To Francis Jammes' is an indispensable mark of loyalty.

> Attendue
> A travers les étés qui s'ennuient dans les cours . . . etc.
> [Expected / through the summers which grow weary in the courtyards]

Nice. The whole stanza is good (maybe a little long), I particularly like:

> Ceux qui rêvaient d'amour
> et qui pleuraient d'enfance.
> [Those who dreamed of love / and who wept for lost childhood]

(In 'Almaïde d'Etrement' there occurs: 'Dans la longueur de ce triste et ancien après-midi.'[2] But that's nothing.)

Especially

> Vous êtes venue
> une après-midi chaude ('après-midi' is masculine)
> [You came along / one hot afternoon]

I'd like to see a comma after 'un peu' to link it by thought to 'sérieux'. I adore 'penché comme mon enfance' [leaning like my childhood]. The final line is very nice too.[3]

*

I don't understand the rest very well. If 'surprise' alludes to Her, the feeling is not made very clear. If it refers to you, I fail to understand

> . . . d'être venue et d'être blonde . . .
> de vous être soudain
> mise
> sur mon chemin
> [for having come and for being blonde . . . for having suddenly / put yourself / in my path]

Don't overdo short and very short lines. They spoil the effect a little bit when their use is not fully justified.
I love:

> Avec, dans vos cheveux, tous les étés du Monde
> [With all the summers of the world in your hair]
> (but no capital M for *monde*)

*

The following stanza just a little banal (the last two lines especially).

*

> et une vieille dame GAIE (?) a votre bras
> [and a gay old lady on your arm]

I was about to observe, wrongly, that the grammatical connection is a bit loose.

> à pas
> lents, un peu, n'est-ce pas, un peu sous votre ombrelle,
> [with slow steps, partly, I think, beneath your parasol]

179

rather Francis Jammes.

*

I very much like the way the following stanza picks up and 'explains' 'A la maison d'été' of the last line of the preceding stanza.
Altogether a very nice stanza. But:

> Dans les livres de prix, monsieur et madame d'Avran
> reviendraient en pressant le pas chez eux,
> vers un château tout bleu, malgré le mauvais temps.
> Le vent.
> [In the prize-books, Monsieur and Madame d'Arvan / would make a hasty retreat home, / towards a castle, all blue despite the bad weather. / The wind.]

and:

> parce que tu lisais, étant tout petite,
> dans les livres de distribution de prix
> que les beaux fiancés se faisaient aimer vite
> [because, as a little child, you used to read / in the prize-books / that handsome couples swiftly fell in love]

and:

> Elle me rappelle les écolières d'alors
> qui avaient des noms rococos, des noms de livres
> de distribution des prix, verts, rouges, olives,
> avec un ornement ovale, un titre en or.
> [She reminds me of the schoolgirls of those days / who had outlandish names, names found in the prize-books / bound in green, red, olive, / with an oval decoration and a title in gold]

I feel ashamed of these merciless quotations, but it is you who insist on my being disagreeable!

*

Very nice again, the stanza: 'Vous entriez là-bas . . .' [You entered there]. But:

> Cela
> fait s'effeuiller . . .
> [That / set the leaves falling]⁴

this present tense following an imperfect is very Jammes, likewise the expression 'Cela fait'.

180

But I'm not criticizing you for it.

Exquisite: 'Et dans l'allée comme un chemin de fête-Dieu' [And in the pathway like a procession on Corpus Christi Day].

＊

The following stanza is also exquisite, especially: 'balaiera des parfums couleur de vos cheveux' [will sweep along perfumes the colour of your hair].

＊

I like the change of rhythm in 'Puis recevoir tous deux,' etc . . . [Then for both to receive]. Very nice the stanza 'Ou bien lire avec vous . . .' [Or else read with you]. Especially

aux roucoulements longs des colombes peureuses
et cachées qui s'effarent de la page tournée
[to the long cooings of the timid, hidden doves / frightened
by the sound of the turning page][4]

But I have a feeling of having read in the *Angélus*, 'à l'heure où l'on entend tirer de l'eau au puits' [at the hour when you hear water drawn at the well].

＊

I love the adorable stanzas: 'C'est là qu'auprès de vous, ô ma lointaine,' etc . . . especially

a ce château dont vous étiez, douce et hautaine,
la châtelaine
[It is there beside you, O my distant beloved . . . in this
castle where you, sweet but remote, / are the châtelaine][4]

The rhythm is exquisitely smooth. I think it is my favourite stanza. I am less enamoured of the final stanza, even with its Jammes-like 'puis', and 'et puis 'près' — and its lovely last line.

Such then is my detailed impression. You must have found it painful and I expect I've left you with the impression of a donkey tramping over a flower-bed. I'm very sorry if I appear to have been insensitive.

I come back to my general impression — that it is indecisive, lacking in conviction. I hesitate before passing judgement. The ambiguity I mentioned at the beginning is a little disturbing. It is a very long section, and, as rhythmic pattern, reminds one a little of those exordia and perorations in the poems of *Tel qu'en songe*, which are set in italics.

> Mon âme s'est songée au miroir
> Que ta main haussait en face des calmes soirs, etc . . .
> [My soul dreamed itself in the mirror / which your hand raised before tranquil evenings]

Now this has nothing to do with Jammes whose phrases are short, tentative, repeated, stammered. And I am surprised to find a very Jammes-like sensibility in the very broad poetic form you adopt.

Nevertheless, for me, it is one of your most delightful poems and it seems to reflect very well what I had sensed in the version you spoke about.

*

A word now about your reading:

WELLS: I think the most interesting thing about him is his discovery of the unexpected romanticism of science. Consequently one should read his novels in which his powerful imagination, neglecting the probable, evokes the possible. The result is often impressive.

J.-A. RIMBAUD. I can't quite make out from your account how you finally assess him. Is it still distaste or a smile of superior indulgence? Please explain, because I am intrigued by this individual whom others have tried to make out to be a genius.

VERHAEREN. You did well to buy the *Campagnes hallucinées*. I've been told or read somewhere that it is his masterpiece. I've written a bit of a diatribe on him to Guéniffey. I like, I venerate him, I find him delightful; but, for all that, I can't bring myself to open his book. The *Angélus* or Régnier's *Poems* always seem to take precedence. For all his power as a great poet, Verhaeren has too many faults, whereas I read *Telqu'un songe de soir et d'espoir* in order to commit it to memory, and every moment brings a precious discovery. I believe that twenty years hence people will talk of Régnier as today they talk of Vigny.

I'm saying this to stir you up a bit.

Various other matters:

VIGIER. He has written to me and I have replied. He wrote to me about English poetry and about philosophy. Neither subject seemed to interest him much, though he likes Rossetti well enough. I replied with a brief lecture on Barrès with whom he seems fairly familiar.

MYSELF. Yes, I'll certainly be coming to Paris in November as a student at the Sorbonne. I am really thrilled about it, although my parents, without wishing to admit it to me, are thinking of dumping me on some distant relatives, which would restrain my freedom. All the same I'm delighted. I've never felt as intensely as I do now how essential it was for me not to return to the 'dump'.

MUSICAL QUESTION. I'm delighted. Camille Mauclair is laying in to Jean Marnold and Louis who are emitting screams of rage!

YOURSELF. You'll find it curious after my telling you: 'Yes, you're right, you must get yourself into print', that I should now be saying 'Yes, you're right, you must NOT be insistent on getting yourself into print'. But my apparent change of opinion will no longer come as a surprise. I believe very strongly that you are quite right not to insist on trying to enter the narrow portals of *l'Ermitage* but to work. Yes, work away assiduously for a year, doing nothing else, with the energy of a locomotive rushing at sixty miles an hour — there is nothing like it. All the more because one year of that stupid régime will suffice for life. In one year you can learn *everything you need to know* — in a word, things of no interest. In one year you win salvation and acquire an indestructible force. It seems worth it, to me. Get on with it then, and may the Lord watch over you!

∗

Although I may be quite out of order, I'd like to add a word or two about Laforgue and Barrès.

LAFORGUE. I've enjoyed re-reading 'Convalescence en Mai'. It has some distichs that greatly appeal to me:

Oh! mort, tout mort au plus jamais, au vrai néant
Des nuits où piaule en longs regrets un chat-huant!

183

Et pourtant le béni grand bol, etc . . .

Voici l'oeuf à la coque et la lampe du soir, etc.[5]

Yet the thing as a whole leaves me cold, uneasy, because of my (very French) need for literary formality. This feeling may well be a little bourgeois, but I'm unable to shake it off. You will say: 'But what wealth of poetry and refinement!' Well, no, I really can't associate myself with this sentiment. I am put off by an incoherence, doubtless intentional, which seems somewhat facile. The associations of ideas make such enormous leaps that I'm left dumbfounded. All this irritates me and interferes with my enjoyment of things which, taken separately, are perhaps very fine. Consequently, I am quite unable to find in it 'a wealth of refinement'.

I am well aware that the poet wanted to give the impression of wild and fugitive dreams of a convalescence, the despair of a sick man who sees his whole life behind him, and before him — he knows not what. And I recall that all the poems of his that I've read have given me this same impression of incoherence — excusable in this case, but not always.

It is probably hurtful to you when I talk in this way about one of your most cherished idols. But I am cultivating the habit of being sincere, that's to say, cruel. Furthermore, people don't come to an understanding only through shared religions, but also through differing beliefs.

To return to this need for formality that I mentioned, it is what causes me to admire so intensely — more than you — Mallarmé's sonnets, where nothing is left to chance, the 'impression' being meticulously composed, where each element makes its contribution and the musical sense, in its authoritative development, helps one to grasp the literary sense. Here, for example, is a sonnet I adore:

Quelle soie aux baumes du temps
Où la Chimère s'exténue
Vaut la torse et native nue
Que hors de ton miroir tu tends.

Les trous de drapeaux méditants
S'exaltent dans notre avenue.

Moi j'ai ta chevelure nue
Pour enfouir mes yeux contents.

Mais la bouche ne sera sûre
De rien goûter à sa morsure
S'il ne fait ton princier amant

Dans la considérable touffe
Expirer comme un diamant
Le cri des gloires qui'il étouffe.[6]

I consider it an example of a very pure and lofty art. But don't hesistate to tear it to shreds — I shall be delighted. It will lessen my feelings of guilt.

BARRÈS. Understanding him so well, I find it very difficult to talk to you about him. At the time of writing, I've read: *Sous l'oeil des barbares. Un Homme libre. Le Jardin de Bérénice. Du sang, de la volupté et de la mort. L'Ennemi des lois.* I shan't stop until I've read the lot.

Obviously, along with *Samson et Dalila*, Debussy and Maeterlinck, he's one of the great revelations of my life.

Barrès is quite different from what you imagine. He is not only 'the most delightful of our insolent writers' (Charles Guérin), he's a sage. I've just finished *L'Ennemi des lois* for the second time and, anticipating your objection (i.e. what about your political theories?), I do hope you'll read it.

But I'm going to stop at this point. I really am unable to say anything about him. State all your objections, let me know which 'philosophical and literary' beliefs you find upsetting in my admiration for him. Then I'll reply.

For the moment, however, I feel ashamed and guilty at having spoken so clumsily of someone who is as subtle and profound as the spirit of fire.

I've forwarded the 15 September number of the *Mercure* to [Guinle] who will, I expect, pass it to you at the start of the new term. You will, won't you, buy the 1 September issue. I need it terribly! I'll catch up with them both in November and read them if I've time. I'm planning to devote October to studying philosophy. An urgent need.

On Tuesday I am setting off for a trip in the Pyrenees and I'll be back on Thursday evening or Friday morning. I won't be

leaving Arcachon definitely before Monday, 1 October.
The bursary business will, I think, be settled on the 10th.
You are certain to see Chesneau before me; he says he has to
be in Paris, early October, to sit his Chartres exam.
All I've had from Guinle is a postcard promising me a letter
which hasn't yet arrived.
At this point I'll stop while waiting for your letter which is
bound to be long and full of interest — all the more so since it
will be the last one you will be able to write in complete
freedom.
I await it with as much eagerness as if I was about to see you
in person and shake you by the hand.

Jacques Rivière

1   The long poem 'A travers les étés' contains the germ of much that was to
be developed in *Le Grand Meaulnes*: recollections of childhood, schooldays
and, above all, the encounter with Yvonne de Quiévrecourt (Yvonne de
Galais of the novel) in Paris — 'ô ma lointaine . . .'.
2   Poem by Jammes: 'during the length of this sad and ancient afternoon'.
3   Fournier kept the lines 'Vous êtes venue . . . mon enfance' unchanged in
the final version, but took Rivière's criticism of the others to heart.
4   The lines marked were retained, the others altered or dropped. In
referring to the châtelaine, Fournier applies the adjective 'hautaine' as he had
to Yvonne after their 1 June encounter.
5   'Oh dead, dead for ever, consigned to true oblivion / of nights when a
tawny owl screeches in drawn-out laments!'; 'And yet the blessed large bowl
. . .'; 'Here is the boiled egg and the evening lamp . . .'.
6   Cecily Mackworth, an authority on Mallarmé, suggested to me that this
poem had never been translated, on account of its difficulty, but has kindly
provided a guide:
'No silk odorous with time / and illusion fading away / can match the breasts
and your pure nudity / you hold out to me through your mirror.
Through the pensive flags in our avenue / the tatters tell of glory / I bury my
satisfied eyes / deep in your unloosed hair.
But this mouth cannot be sure / to have known the full taste / till your
princely lover / has exhaled like a diamond / the cry of glory he stifles / In the
luxuriant mass.'

22 September 1905   *Paris*

My dear Jacques,
    Back in France since Sunday evening.
    Will write to you *tomorrow morning* — about *Mélanges posthumes*, Jammes, and *Villes tentaculaires* in particular.
    Wait for this letter before replying to my previous two, if you haven't already replied to the first.
    I'm leaving for Nançay on Monday with the *Pro Archia* in my pocket. Will send some ghastly postcards.

                                                                    Henri

Le Deuil des primevères: seventeen elegies — six 'evocative' poems ('Mme de Warens', 'Guadeloupe de Alcaras', etc.) — two character-machines like 'Un Jour: Le Poète et l'Oiseau' — 'La Jeune Fille nue' — and *Quatorze prières* (amongst which: 'Prière pour aller au Paradis avec les ânes', 'Prière pour avoir une femme simple', 'Prière pour demander une étoile . . .')
    The *Mélanges* together with *Lettres* and *Critique d'art* above all.

23 September 1905   *La Chapelle d'Angillon (Cher)*

My dear Jacques,
    Despite a sore throat and running head cold, I am sacrificing this splendid morning of my brief vacation to tell you a whole heap of things.

ENGLAND

I left it last Saturday at ten o'clock in the evening.
    In the course of a final conversation with Mr Nightingale, I told him that I had always thought of him as the ideal gentleman. He replied by way of some grave, sincere and considered compliments. We parted quite moved — like a couple of

friends. At the last moment as the train drew out, we both raised our hats — an emotional, almost mutually respectful gesture. In a way, Mr Nightingale had always symbolized England for me.

And I departed — after leaving him — deeply moved in spite of the pleasure of going home, leaving the great bridges 'thrown in leaps' across the Thames, as described by Verhaeren — the sea of roofs with their lighted windows above which we flew to a rattle of iron — all this vast city, joyfully lit up on that Saturday night, only to collect itself and brood in silence the whole of the next day — all this I had first come upon one sparkling July morning, green and fresh in the morning sun when, landing on the island, it seemed to me like landing on another planet. And now all this, veiled in September mist, as winter approaches, I leave with an enormous attachment.

I must tell you that towards the end they once again increased my wages — I was earning £2.8s a month! And they are to transcribe my commercial translations to use as models! It seems I am leaving behind an excellent impression among these machine-men to whom I've always shown a machine-like coolness. I'm pleased to have proved that, if I wanted, I could acquit myself more than honourably at one of these ordinary jobs in everyday business life.

I saw my English girl who might be considered pretty by anyone else but me. Physically very different from what I'd imagined. Charmingly respectable and very much as I'd imagined. There must be some lovely girls in England, but they are rather free-and-easy. Mine took me off for an hour to a quiet corner of Hyde Park where we sat side by side under an oak tree. In front of us, a vast expanse of green, dotted about with oak-trees — just like a meadow in Berri — but as far as the eye can see. Even a few deer — and yet we were in the heart of London, myself and a girl! I felt as if I was living in the Country of the Transmutation of all values!

She must have been surprised at finding me so cold and reserved — so different from what she must have imagined and what people here imagine all Frenchmen to be like.

Amongst other things, I've brought back from England the English scorn of Frenchmen as small men with moustaches and goatee beards, quite incapable of controlling either their tongues or their affairs.

I stopped off in Paris only for a single hour — a formidable trial. With my mind a blank, I travelled with my trunk in an open cab from the Gare Saint-Lazare to the Quai d'Orsay. Once there, the Seine, the quays, the bridges — all inspired some delightful thoughts . . .

At nine o'clock in the morning, I had a drunken cab-driver who more than once nearly smashed me to pieces and who, despite my frantic hurry, managed to run into a traffic-jam, then a crowded street-market, then a dead-end! It was Sunday morning and everybody was in good spirits and jeered at him with incredible verve! Everybody addressed me with incredible gaiety! I nearly died of laughter over this Paris welcome.

At about three o'clock in the afternoon, I rediscovered France — at Bourges where I had a two hours' wait. I ate a galette at the pastry-shop in the Avenue de la Gare, next to 'Lavex — Footwear of every kind'. A quiet Sunday afternoon in September, but with sunshine as warm as in summer yet as fresh as in springtime. I took a right turn into a deserted boulevard along one side of which extend all the gardens of Bourges. It was entirely green, criss-crossed with paths over-hung with fruit trees. All the benches covered with dust. The town rose up towards the lycée and the cathedral. When I was a schoolboy walking these pavements, my sweethearts used to be listening to the band playing; now they were doubtless strolling along, one with a white sunshade, another with blue eyes . . . But where? A man, two men passed by carrying a basket of peaches . . .

My heart was too full not to find an outlet in a poem — this is the result — so please tear it up.

Unused as I was to my surroundings back here, I found everything more familiar, more rural — the roads with their hedges and grass verges all green as I now observe and, quite close in the hollows cottage roofs at road level. All that so close and yet so extensive. Endless little lanes — endless lanes between hedges.

*

If I was writing to myself, I would stop at this point or else chat about the coming term and the Cagne.

In fact I've made up my mind to lose myself in the good earth and sky, to eat like a horse for this fortnight (more than a week anyhow), to tone up my muscles — maxillary and motory — and then go back to the Cagne like a good boy.

Besides, to my great surprise, I find I've always been prepared to sacrifice Laforgue, Jammes and Verhaeren for 'a walk by Neuvy-deux-Clochers and Presly-le-Chétif'. Improbable though it may appear, the fact remains that after one week, only the Jammes — of my three books — is nearly finished.

However, I want to get a few items off my chest — literary and otherwise — which I had to tell you about before leaving for Nançay.

I enclose a poem of mine: the one about September and the little old lady. There is also a little old lady in *La Jeune Fille nue*,[1] which is irritating — she was so very much my own, this old lady, but when it comes down to it, it doesn't really matter. You'll notice the development of my *vers libre* which I've already talked to you about.

Also a vague poem which seems more like a notation in the manner of 'Trois heures', 'Dimanche des Rameaux'. I should add that the poem was conceived after 'A travers les étés'.

That's all I've managed, I've got some rough notes for future — or not so future — novels and a piece that I've begun, an outcome of 'A travers les étés' part of something which could be called: 'Un roman de province' or 'Un roman d'autrefois' — or nothing at all. Doubtless it will not be completed until very much later on.

✻

In the meantime, I need to develop my intellect, although I have the most profound contempt for the intellect or what passes for it. I'm thinking here a great deal about the kind of intelligence which very justifiably describes *Le Visage émerveillé* as 'Sensual Mysticism' or that which stated that the earth turns on its axis or that invented the syllogism!

All that seems to me absolutely useless or announced *post hoc* and fallacious!

I think, too, of the relativity of human intelligence and of the intelligence displayed by Barrès and the 'Barbarians' being almost identical.

I believe all lives are worth living. One evaluates them, despising some, glorifying others perhaps because, in an arbitrary manner one sees them as fragments of a whole, of a society or an ideal — something which has no more justification for existing than anything else.

On reflection, I approve of this notion of assuming a mask, social or any other kind in a society imposed on one. That is to say this searching for a means of living one's own life calmly and not a life which others impose on one in the interests of some ideal or other.

But you haven't either any right to treat your ideal — your ideal world — as the only reasonable and valid one or to dub Barbarians those who do not contribute to it.

I believe that the best wisdom consists of understanding everything and then of loving everything. For others this means understanding everything and then of making comparisons and being superior. I am disgusted with those who refuse to understand and only mock — or like Nietzsche — insult. And this is what passes for philosophy!

I, too, have a liking for irony although, in the final analysis, this is no more than by way of stating how insignificant I feel myself to be, and what little progress in life I have made!

Nevertheless, it seems to me that all this is nothing but a polite formula — just another way of deceiving, at some stage in one's progress, those in whose company one mixed! After all, something more is required in order to advance. Scepticism spells cessation, death. For a time it can destroy, after that its function ends. I don't know much about Barrès, but it appears to me that more often than not he applies his scepticism only in his political crises and that I find deplorable. And when he had done with complaining, he hooked himself on to Alsace-Lorraine. To go forward, it seems you've got to believe that 'something has happened'. In this sense each of us, unconsciously has his presiding Deity. Le Chevallier and Gotteland believe in academic honours; Chotard and Marchand in the Republic; Marchand in socialism, another in money, another in his heart. One says: I believe only what I understand — another: what I feel — another: what I see . . . etc. etc. It is worth noting that delinquents, imbeciles — the most barbarian of barbarians who appear to deride everything and believe in nothing — are those who are the most convinced that 'it's happened'. Only, this something that's happened that people discover sooner or later and for which they sacrifice everything else, doesn't interest me, that's all there is to it. All it amounts to is social or academic success or money, etc . . .

Perhaps I should be joining you and Barrès if I were to say that by the time you've got to the stage of understanding everything, you notice that *nothing* has happened — and that the imbeciles are the ones that believe it has all happened. Imbeciles, that is, perhaps, *imbecilles* in Latin.

That is why, at the beginning of the paragraph, I stated that before embarking on an important, serious work, I wanted to become less of an ignoramus.

✻

I'm holding a handkerchief to my running nose in my left hand — and I told you once for all that I considered this business of setting things out in formulas absolutely hopeless.

However, this doesn't prevent my finding your points about ideology delightful, precisely because I am not qualified to make them myself — and they certainly need to be made.

As for me, I will always prefer to stop and talk about the 'dazzlingly blue Mediterranean' — or the harvester I can hear roaring away in the fields behind me as if to tell me that it is still summer — still a little bit left out of all this summer that I've not lived.

✻

I've been to see *Hamlet*. Token scenery, bad acting, but I enjoyed seeing it done like that.

Did I tell you that during the first weeks in London I went to a wretched hen-house of a theatre and saw a melodrama, complete with poisonings, hangings, murders, treachery and terror — to the accompaniment of hissing, howling from a terrified audience, in turn weeping or roaring with laughter.

That is what *Hamlet* is really about. On this occasion, it was a different kind of audience — and yet they come along in the same spirit in which they would attend a contemporary play, and, by Jove, they certainly got their money's worth of terror,

192

horrid thoughts, macabre scenes and bawdy jests.

We were treated to a ghost to dream about at night. There was a throne-room complete with a coat-of-arms in the form of three ravens! As melodrama, *Hamlet* is a masterpiece.

In the last scene, they are all on stage, being killed off — crying out and bleeding to death! Only the King is left, who lunges forward with sword drawn to defend himself against Hamlet. The Prince, twisting round and roaring with laughter, seizes a fish-net, throws it over the King's head and runs him through as nice as you please!

The part of Hamlet was taken by a tall strapping fellow, continually ranting, aggrieved and frightened — acting atrociously, but in my opinion, very naturalistically.

All this reminds me that I once expressed my scepticism to you regarding the symbols and truths hidden in ancient tragedies.

I was mistaken. Both *Hamlet* and *Oedipus* are human 'passions' expressed on one occasion and in one particular way. To say that the dramatist has expressed what Laforgue or you and I, moderns, see in it, would be a foolish observation. Nevertheless, we have every right to see it in whatever we do, for, over the centuries, from Sophocles to Shakespeare to ourselves, passion and grief are always the *same*, but enriched through those who experience them, becoming more refined, more subtle (I interpret the terms 'passion', 'grief', etc in the broadest possible sense). Therefore one is always justified in making Antigone a symbol of filial piety for example, giving it its fullest significance — one is always justified, one is always right in taking a quotation from *Hamlet* as an epigraph.

✻

The epigraphs one can glean, even harvest, in Rimbaud are quite another matter. He has put into them everything you care to find but he has not had the courage to formulate them himself.

Any fool would be right to consider Rimbaud stupid; I find enormous pleasure in doing so myself.

In a word, his book, all his books are incomplete.

Of course, they can't be completed since what he has expressed as best he can, is fixed once for all, and, all the same, one can't now go back to the phase from his *Poésies* up to *Une Saison en enfer*. It was for this reason that I said he belonged to his own time; that's all there is to it.

I have written out for you what I consider to be characteristic examples of his different styles.

Poésies — from the age of fifteen to seventeen — in the Coppée manner[2] plus a taste for the macabre and repellent.

Poésies — second period when he attempts (what everyone should try once in his poetic career) to write poetry about everything (impromptu and the rest) quite sincerely.

Les Illuminations. Premières and *Secondes Illuminations*. A collection of reflections, visions above all (whence perhaps Paterne Berrichon's affection for them)[3], and especially of sensations. Whole pages of short sayings which give you goose-flesh. Ten-line visions that are bouts of madness one fears to see become contagious.

Basically, there's no real harm in all this. From time to time he calms down and becomes converted to Beauty, to the Good Lord etc.

In *Une Saison en enfer* he reviews his life; complains, cries over it, giving everyone the impression — which has become an accredited legend — that he was a pederast and, when all's said and done, a fine fellow and something of an oddity.

Our mellifluous friend Paterne Berrichon holds forth about his admirable life.

During the years immediately preceding his death, it appears that he refused to countenance any mention of his work. When the subject happened to come up, he was invariably heard to say: idiotic! absurd! disgusting! Only the *Illuminations* were published with his consent and the day after publication he had the whole edition burnt.

Remind me to talk to you later — in Paris — about:
1. An obsession with Laforgue-Rimbaud that I consider very right and proper.
2. An obsession with 'Laforgue-Rimbaud and others' that I've discovered which is puerile; besides Laforgue discovered it before (or after) me (and noted it in his *Critiques littéraires*).

✳

Following my (more than adequate) reading of the three books you know about, it seems to me that Verhaeren, Jammes and Laforgue have gone off in different directions from mine and that (come now! so much the better) they have not said all that needs to be said and that I myself intend to say.

Hence an initial disappointment. The 'so much the better', followed by a feeling of immense sympathy and admiration — especially for the first works which brought me to the knowledge and appreciation of these writers.

✳

As for Laforgue's *Letters* — some are exquisite. Most of all those written to his sister, Marie. She must have been a rather unremarkable provincial woman, all the same, his sister. I started from his premise and found Laforgue much as I had imagined — with not a few of my own obsessions — his wanting to snip off a small piece of wallpaper from his sordid room to send to his sister, etc. And just listen to his carrying on about his shirts and money-orders! You should read the letter in which he tells how he feeds himself — as *we* used to before *Pelléas* — on bread rolls and brawn. This includes his purchase of some brawn, nervously, blushingly — an epic in itself! It makes you smile but with tears in your eyes (nor does he have to play the man-of-letters with his sister).

And then his marriage with the English girl before he has even shaken her hand! Exquisite. He doesn't dare use her name, calling her 'le petit personnage'.

The rest was disappointing. Why does the poor fellow allow himself to be distracted by such stupidities as the earth's rotation, the life of the planets, the detritus of life, the sordidity of the human body etc. Why had not his idealism cured him of all that?

What he describes as his great epic on Pierrot is called *Pierrot Fumiste* who marries but is unable to bring himself to 'possess' Colombinette. All this, to borrow your phrase, is 'of no great interest'. It is the kind of preoccupation one has, especially at the age of twelve. Jammes and idealism are the cure. His notes on Impressionism, art and literature are very impressive. But it is no longer my Laforgue.

I am transcribing his fine *Rêve de rose* for you and adding something of my own.

195

I am trying to think how it occurred to me to buy Rimbaud. In the *Mercure* catalogue I had noticed: *Lettres de Jean-Arthur Rimbaud* (Egypt — Arabia — Ethiopia). Being myself something of a traveller, I was tempted to know what those countries had meant to so strange a being. Then I had said to myself 'I might as well start by getting to know his works'.

✻

Verhaeren: *Les Villes tentaculaires*, followed by *Campagnes hallucinées*. Its major shortcoming: lack of variety.

I can perhaps forgive him for being permanently uncivilized, for never tiring at ending each stanza with 'immensity', 'infinitely', 'athwart', 'towards one knows not what', 'from one end of the world to the other' . . . But his very subject, even with these restraints, makes him look as if the idea of Town enticing Country had occurred to him one day and persuaded him to develop it through poems — pages and pages of them.

'La Ville', 'à la Bourse', 'à l'Etal', in the 'Usines' or the 'Bazar'. It's always something noisy, dissolute, hazy; as for his 'Campagne' — he has felt obliged to show it at its last gasp amid epidemics, superstitions, horror, in order to better explain the exodus to the City.

The whole thing ends with the apotheosis of Ideas and Inventions.

Of course there are some splendid though not novel pieces which add nothing to his reputation. He has not renewed his technique — always the same alliteration, imitative harmony, etc . . .

I'm very taken with the opening of his latest poem in the *Mercure*: '. . . passent à l'horizon ainsi que des montagnes'.

✻

Jammes: *Le Deuil des primevères*. With a short preface explaining that despite appearances to the contrary, he is not even remotely worried about pleasing certain critics; that his form is geared to his sensation, be it excitable or tranquil; that *Le Deuil des primevères* is calm in form and content above all because it led him into a solitude where his suffering was occasionally appeased; and that furthermore, his collection is to be followed by a book entitled *Poésie*, which would better underline his

196

development.

Naturally, I cannot even think of comparing it with the *Angélus*. I immediately seemed to find faults of which I was already half aware: 'Too much refinement. Too self-consciously simplistic'. But perhaps I'm wrong. Only yesterday I adored it. How can one criticize a true poet? His poems are merely 'those winged and subtle dreams whose secret he holds'. How beautiful, the first elegy: 'A Samain', written after Samain's death! And then the second and all the others. I like 'Sa Mamore' as much perhaps as 'Amaryllis'.

Reply soon.

Yours

Henri

P.S. Tell me if you have any chance of sending these poems on to Guéniffey.

1 *La Jeune Fille nue* (1899), by Francis Jammes; the line from 'A travers les étés' to which Fournier refers is: 'Et une vieille dame gaie à votre bras . . .'.

2 François Coppée (1842–1908), lyric poet, many of whose poems deal with humble life.

3 Berrichon was Rimbaud's brother-in-law, and wrote his biography through disapproving of his life.

26 September 1905   *Arcachon*

Dear Henri,

Ah! but I really have something to say to you now.

You see, it's very difficult to understand Barrès when you haven't read everything (I mean Barrès before *Les Déracinés*, which forms a whole). You make the same mistake I committed when I passed judgement on him after reading *Sous l'oeil des barbares* and from which *Un Homme libre* had scarcely liberated me. But you have to read the lot. *Le Jardin de Bérénice* and especially *L'Ennemi des lois* will give you some delightful surprises.

Barrès is not one to stand before the Barbarians as if he alone was of any interest. For him the term 'barbarian' does not have a pejorative sense. He says: 'The Barbarians are the non-self'. He calls them Barbarians because, like anyone else, he has suffered at their hands, from their animosity, their opposition to the development of his 'self' — his ego. It is *impossible*, don't you think, not to be infuriated at some point with this unconscious and disturbing mass we call 'the others'. It is the majority he qualifies as 'Barbarians'. And he claims that one's first duty is to break away from the influence of these philistines and cultivate one's ego scrupulously, to develop one's personality, refusing all constraints and end up a free man, that is to say, completely unprejudiced and able to live intensely, feeding on noble and precious emotions.

But wait — that's not everything! If such a man stays shut within himself he can be wonderfully intelligent and so self-aware that he can regulate his soul like a watchmaker a clock, know all the cogs and make it mark the hour he wants. But he will very quickly tire of this over-intellectual, over-intelligent life.

Therefore he goes back to the Barbarians and endeavours to find in them the power of the unconscious, the continuous and unending supply of energy. To whom is he to address himself? Not to the middle-brows, whose indifferent education has merely changed their prejudices (Marchand, Chotard, etc), nor to 'the engineer, Charles Martin', who would have us govern the unconscious by mathematical and ruthless laws, nor to the 'Adversary'; — but to Bérénice as she bends in tears over a dead love — Bérénice, who personifies the *people*, who have not yet come of age, but develop slowly in accordance with secret but immutable laws. It is in Bérénice, it is in the people that the free man will seek inner strength, the enduring energy which will unify his over-intelligent, over-diversified ego.

And yet, to this extent he is still not perfectly happy since he cannot be happy all alone. Which leads him on to this: 'The free man can find happiness only in the happiness of others. Other "selfs" exist to the same degree as his own, so that the conditions of other people's happiness should merge into the conditions of his own.' But Barrès then notes that the laws which were originally made to guarantee the minimum injustice possible, reached the point of consecrating crimes and stifling real virtue. So they had to be suppressed (*L'Ennemi des lois*), and, after the period of socialism, indispensable for the perfecting of material life (without which all spiritual life is impossible), after this period, we will have recourse to anarchy, the supreme remedy to all evils, since by suppressing the general ego from which the laws emanate, it will leave each individual self free to develop unharmed.

Doubtless he sets it before us only as a Utopia, but then surely it is a sublime utopia and one to which we are all already converted. The sole difference between Barrès and ourselves is that he, it appears, leaves it to natural evolution which, for our part, we would prefer to speed up. And then he is not really sure of his faith and I, likewise doubt that I believe (as is my right), since I behave as if I was certain about things, and act accordingly.

You can see how far all this is from the idea you appear to have of Barrès. Now, it is certain that we feel ourselves to be a bit above the Barbarians. Yet, is there not a kind of inner hypocrisy involved when we equate ourselves with the lowest kind of imbecile, when we affirm that we have nothing more to ourselves than he has? It's all very nice expressed in words, but are we ever really convinced? Oh! I believe only in the absolute, and if there is a God, then in His eyes I'm worth no more than the fool just because, at birth, I was given the gift of intelligence. In practice, it doesn't stop me from putting a slightly higher value on myself if only because of the services I am capable of rendering. Besides, in what way does my pride hurt anyone provided I keep it to myself?

Here I touch on the most valuable lesson that I've learned from Barrès and the signal service he has done me. For some time — partly under Mélinand's influence — I had been attaching importance only to what seemed to belong to my reason, as a rational or reasonable being. I had been neglecting or stifling through sheer prejudice the manifold subtleties which I was unable to justify on rational grounds and which I deemed to be of no use. That is why I increasingly avoided coarse talk and obscene allusions. It pained me, but I was reluctant to admit it, believing that decency in all its forms was irrational. (Hence my harangue at Easter — which I now disown.) Barrès has taught me to 'discriminate between what shocks my prejudices and what really offends my susceptibilities'. He has taught me to keep a more watchful eye on my moral standards and to 'compose' myself more. An inestimable benefit; I am already feeling its full effects.

Barrès came along just when I had need of him, and it is almost a blessing that I misunderstood him so long. And since, added to the benefits I derive from reading him is one of the deepest aesthetic pleasures I have ever experienced, you see what a debt I owe him.

Hence these four pages which I've written in one go, almost as soon as I received your letter.

There remains the question of scepticism which you state admirably, even though you are wrong in saying that it 'spells cessation, death'. Like you, I believe that everyone has his divinity. I think it necessary to have a good God of one's own, only one should not exaggerate one's belief. We should realize that we arbitrarily blind ourselves. Those who don't know this are to be pitied and I'm sorry for them. They are the Barbarians. Yes, the 'imbeciles' in the Latin sense. But how could you say that someone who believes in socialism, or academic distinction or in money is as good as the next man who believes in nothing, yet behaves as if he believes in justice? It really is a bit steep to interfere in this way in the personal beliefs of others and state that a believer, of whatever sort, and whatever he does, is better than someone who behaves well and is (in the broadest sense) an *atheist*. That is just Christian superstition.

My only faith is that the great truth consists in not believing and to behave solely in ways that conform to beauty (which in a certain sense is not as amoral as one thinks).

'To understand everything and to love everything', you say. It's what I say, too. To understand everything, that is to say, realizing that nothing is certain. To love everything, that is to say, stripping wretchedness of its horror through a deep understanding of it and discovering its beauty (cf. *L'Ennemi des lois*). We are in total agreement, my dear friend! The proof is that we join forces in our scorn for Nietzsche, a denouncer in short, who 'reviles without trying to comprehend'. He's another one who drives you mad with his transmutations. Fancy imagining that changing values will bring about anything but a topsy-turvy world!

That apart, a poet.

*

I have still a deal more to pronounce on the subject, but I'm stopping, for I must post this letter before setting out on my travels and I would like to say a word or two on other subjects.

YOUR POEMS: I like them very much indeed. I think 'La petite vieille' almost perfect. Much more than in 'A travers les étés', I feel you have mastered *vers libre*; you make it give what you want, you lead it where you want and it begins to adapt itself to your sensibility almost to perfection. It is no longer disconcerting, first because you have more or less banished every trace of Jammes, next because . . . because you handle it better. The end is marvellous.

No less marvellous is the ending of the other poem, despite the fact that the final lines are a little obscure because one doesn't at first realize that *dans les voitures à ânes*, etc . . . depends on: *s'en revenir*.

I like the rest of the poem as much, with *les flambées de grand matin* and *les images et les chromos* and the infinitive: *qu'on verra tout l'hiver . . . représenter . . .* , and *les belles dames avec des manchons et des fourrures dans des paysages de neige*.

I see in all this the beneficial influence Verhaeren has had on you. You have assimilated him so well, and, as you have observed his weaknesses, you have steered clear of them.

201

May I add, to wind up, that certain stanzas of 'A travers les étés', though less perfect, affect me more because the inspiration seems more profound and more genuine?

*

Your final impressions of England and your return to France are delightful and for me, having somehow never felt deeply attached to my own country, almost moving.

*

I share your views on *Hamlet*. I believe Shakespeare intended it as a melodrama. However, I think we are right to put into it all that we see, and that true genius consists in building up a framework on a sufficiently grand scale to allow future generations to accommodate their vision in it.

But I also think that we have all (myself especially) been too derisive about melodrama. In the final scene, as you describe it in performance, I perceive a beauty of truculence and butchery that only the mealy-mouthed could find offensive.

Our French taste, so refined and anodyne as to be unable to accept anything excessive, is admirable, provided it can abdicate on occasion to allow us to enjoy more violent beauties than our own. So long live Shakespeare the great architect of melodrama! And long live too, our intelligence and sensibility which embrace such a wide variety!

*

Thanks for the Rimbaud. I can see it from here. I shall see better when I'm in Paris.

*

Thanks for Laforgue. What a strange idea to be buying his *Mélanges posthumes*. Whilst waiting for the rest, I suppose.

Thanks for Verhaeren. You found the chink in his armour straight away — that lack of variety. It's all the same. When you've read one, you've read the lot. And then all those *Dites! immensément*, etc . . . !

Nevertheless, the strongest impression he makes on me is in this vast work, these thousands of accumulated lines all emitting the same cry of distress, proclaiming the same torment, the

202

same terror. It becomes great through sheer obstinate monotony.

*

The case of Jammes distresses me a great deal. I had already felt anxious about *Le Triomphe de la vie*. I had hoped that *Le Deuil des primevères* would turn out to be a second masterpiece. The two poems you sent me are all very charming, the titles even more, whilst nothing could be sweeter than a poem from *L'Angélus*.

Conclusion: How difficult it is going to be to renew oneself when poets like Verhaeren, Régnier, Jammes and perhaps even Maeterlinck haven't brought it off — successfully I mean. What a terrible lesson!

You must write to me before you leave or on arrival at the 'dump'. In the second case you must give me a description of the new Cagne. In spite of everything I'm still interested.

It's now eleven o'clock; and, with a parting handshake I'm off to bed.

Jacques R.

P.S. Guinle wrote to me in the end and is going to write to you. Not a word out of Guéniffey for a whole month.

26 September 1905   *Nançay*

Dear Jacques,
    Thank you.
    I don't expect to have a spare minute to reply to your letter
before the 1st. How about you?
    I've been reading some analyses *Le Jardin de Bérénice*, etc.,
which showed up some of the stupid things I've said about
Barrès and Alsace-Lorraine. But I have no regrets.
    A lot to say in my replies to you which you will receive
during November or next year.
    Your affectionate friend
                                                    Henri F.

Après-midi: masc. no record of it as feminine (Dictionnaire
Littré) Après midi: masc. or fem. (Dictionnaire de l'Académie)[1]

1   Fournier is perhaps referring back here to Rivière's correction of a line in
'A travers les étés', see letter no. 40.

Vendredi matin. 8/9 05.

Mon cher Jacques.

Cea n'est pas une réponse à ta lettre —
qui n'est pas encore arrivée.
Ce c'est pour te demander un et même
plusieurs services :

Je me suis décidé, en me mettant à
traîner l'Anglais plus dur, à partir le 16
pour me refaire un peu la santé dans
les chantres de Cologne. Je ne me
sens donc plus que 8 jours jusqu'
ne faire un peu une idée de que tout
les théâtres et concerts qui commencent
à se rouvrir.

Le Grand Concert, le Colonne-Lamoureux
de là-bas : c'est Queen's Hall. J'y
suis allé chez hier-soir. j'y retrouverai
peut-être demain soir une Vigie qui
va venir passer la journée à Londres,
J'y retournerai sûrement Lundi
Soir, la séance étant intitulée
"Wagner Night" et comportant le programme
que voici :

[côté gauche de la feuille]

maintenant juste le temps de
avant le courrier étranger le matin qu'il
y ait au programme d'hier soir (celui aussi cher)
Valse de Mephisto — Liszt
Concerto de Rubinstein
Ouverture d'Obéron — Weber
et l'Ouverture de Tannhäuser.
Ce dernier oublié dans ç connaîtrais
Aussi comme une brute.

Donne mon adresse
approximative au Libraire
Larousse.

Mais ne change à le soir
sur du vers que je veux t'envoyer
prochainement — comme je
n'ai qu'à te revoir en Octobre
à Paris. Te recrivai prochainement.

Amitiés. Excuses pour
cette fin à la Galuga.

Henri.

Appendix: I

TO MARIE AND AUGUSTE FOURNIER

7 October 1907

My Dears,
   Thank you all for this morning's letter. I will reply on Monday.
   Can you send me *immediately* a permission 'to allow me leave of absence on Sundays at 11 a.m.' addressed to the Headmaster before next Sunday without fail? Useless to give explanations: a mere formality.
   Thank you, kisses.

Henri

P.S. I'm begining to work like a donkey and to enjoy my work — or I try to do so.
(Written in the chemistry lab. at Lakanal. I didn't know of its existence before.)

This postcard shows how anxious Fournier was to arrange meetings with Jacques in Paris, and how seriously he had taken his friend's advice to work hard in the 'cagne' class.

Appendix: II

Fournier jotted down for himself an account of his seeing and following Yvonne de Quiévrecourt, transcribed here. I have spelt out the words he occasionally abbreviated: the phrases in square brackets were those crossed out in the original manuscript.

'If you had come back when you were supposed to return, I would not have imagined, written this novel about you, Anne-Marie.'

⁜

... as if after a momentary hesitation — a detour — she vanishes behind a group of people, an omnibus, drivers and then, suddenly there she is on my pavement, on the pavement along which I advance quite slowly towards her as she quickens her pace. Three or four persons around us pass by — and here I am as in the cloud of her lace, the boa on her dress, and I say to her as I pass very close in a tone of voice I shall never recapture, so close that she hears, so quickly as she moves past, and completely spontaneously 'You are beautiful'. She has passed by — I think she is at her door, that she is going in, that she has disappeared, and, without properly realizing what I have done, I reach the pavement, over there on the left, the flower-girl's patch of the pavement, where I slowly turn round, where I wait for the window — it is now that I shall know, it is the moment, the window does not open — I walk on ten yards and turn round, the window does not open — and then, all of a sudden, there SHE is coming out opposite me, walking quickly, gazing resolutely in front of her.

I whisper to myself: Fate! the whole of my fate (one exaggerates when one talks to oneself aloud) that [is going to take] is entering the omnibus office — where is she going? this Sunday morning full of the cries of flower-sellers and sunshine and summer dresses returning from mass, summer dresses on their way to mass, [in summer dresses] off (somewhere) to lunch. Is she off to lunch somewhere? I wait on [this] my pavement because — for her — I am afraid of the window. The tram. She gets in and I follow — As I mount the three steps my gaze on hers which she averts and fixes elsewhere, faintly amused, but very dignified, terribly dignified — Here I am on the platform. My thoughts are wandering. I would like to catch a glimpse of her skirt. When is she going to get down(?). I think I can see her hand. My mind has become a blank. It is always the same Sunday and she is getting into the tram and alighting from it to go shopping for her young ladies' dresses or négligés — endless, endless, where is she going to alight? — question.

Now she is setting down — so smoothly in her long [and her] brown train — that I have to be careful not to tread on — a few steps along the pavement and I am close by her and on her right and at first unmoved unaware of what I am doing, unaware, I say to her: 'Tell me you forgive me for having said you were beautiful — for having followed you so long . . .'
— 'But, Monsieur! . . . It's no matter . . .'
Oh in a cutting tone! in a small, firm and disdainful voice — that leaves me stunned and crestfallen — [which puts her among the handsome young ladies who go out unaccompanied . . . and myself, in the street — stunned and crestfallen].
She goes on her way . . . crosses the square.

Sceaux — 17 June 1905

A few yards on and I'm near her again. She doesn't look at me. She looks straight in front of her, her head slightly raised, her neck slightly bent — And I say to her:
'Now that you have said what had to be said, it's finished, you will never say another word, it is completely finished, isn't it?'
— 'But . . . what's the good . . . (a small, very gentle and very firm voice with a faint stress on each syllable — less though still very distant) . . . I leave tomorrow . . . I don't belong to Paris . . .' — a glance, very blue and heart-breaking — and I say 'then I would be glad at least if you will forgive me, Mademoiselle — that you will forgive me for having annoyed,

troubled you.' Oh! then, very sure of herself and of what she is saying, emphasizing the words as if she was defending someone:

'You haven't annoyed me . . . you have behaved very respectfully, I do not bear you any ill will at all . . . I forgive you.' (All this — the end of everything — very finally said as.) The very last word, stated imperceptibly rather solemnly as one says words one believes to be the last. I bow and take my leave in a deeply respectful manner . . . She hurries on to the omnibus office. I can still see her broad-brimmed pink hat through the window — less clearly her blonde, childish, expressive head.

And haughty with it all as if slightly confused, making her seem nevertheless slender and tall and evoking the effect of pretty things which pretty though they are fail to give any idea of the slenderness and elegance of a body beyond all dreams.

Now, a terrible moment, as you can imagine.

She emerges and waits by the kerb for a tram which will not be long coming. There's no help for it. I cross over, I'm about to ruin everything. I make a detour behind some trees and here I am on her right — the whole boulevard stretches before us, St Germain-des-Près — persist. 'I am wrong, am I not, to be insistent?' (Today, this instant, I have just recalled her reply.) At first she made the same impression on me (as) of a pretty nasty, haughty and final leave-taking. I believe rather [however]. It was more or less this [It's useless]. What's the good? — I told you before that I am going away. It is finished now. Oh! I nod a: yes — yes — in what must be a heart-breaking way — and I move off — respectfully — a few steps as I painfully endeavour on this pavement edge to think up some inspired ideas which spring up less than ever.

She pronounces this in a small, uniform, unchanging tone with a slight stress on each word, saying the last one more gently, more drawn-out [more unch] still, slightly detaching the 'g' of 'what's the g   ood?' without moving her head or shifting her gaze and re-assuming afterwards her still more inflexible expression, biting her lips slightly and with her blue eyes gazing straight ahead, unchanging, fixed, blue. I can still hear this voice, I have just repeated 'what's the good' to myself and assumed her tranquil, childlike pose, unchanging and blue, for the hundredth time and repeated, raising my head slightly

210

on the 'g   good' — and I see her again, I hear her and I feel a
desire to bite off my hands because I'm unable to say it.

In her black shoes so open and feminine she has feet with
such slender ankles that sometimes they [bend] give way under
her body and one is afraid of seeing them break.

We are children, we have acted foolishly. You are writing . . . ?
where will you write —
                        and her unbelievable waist
a tiny tear in the lower part of her brown skirt.

                                *

I would only wish to be believed when I say that she was so
beautiful that there cannot be anyone more beautiful in the
world.
Impossible and remote
                        and fugitive
Each explanation of her beauty is an idea and each one is true.
What height had I not then reached when I gained it
    And yet she is someone very special who has no advice to
take from me.
                    nothing could have been more appropriate when
I said 'And your spirit of ancient satin'
    The belfry of Saint Germain-des-Prés, lit up by the moon-
light is silhouetted like a village belfry against a night sky, vast
as over a village.
    The great Adventure

                                *

. . . The eternal Clitandre[1] . . . their long trailing dresses . . .
their soft blue shadows . . .
    It was like a soul perpetually with me. I had almost entirely
forgotten her face. But I know she was there and who she was.
I took her with me everywhere and in her presence nothing
more was hard to bear . . .
    Armed with her love I despised and loved everything.
There was her aloofness — and my love
                    her grace — and my strength.
We were alone in the midst of the world.
we were alone in the midst of the world.
[presentiment]

211

At present I am alone, with the harsh sordid everyday life. It all becomes once more the pain that it was.

2 or 3 letters
Yesterday it seemed to me that merely to cross the bare courtyard without her was painful. She is no longer there. I am alone.

— 'There are others, *more beautiful, more beautiful souls*. This one small, slight, one — There are the souls; you are asking for all the souls, a soul more beautiful than all the other souls. Do you want her? You must not weep.'
I shake my head and want to weep.
About everything, passionately, until the mirage melts away in my hands. They offer me God.

✢

eyes, one evening somewhere else, a hint of the smile, a hint of the lips, of the hair, how shall I remember?
A dream: rows of women, young, beautiful, file past. One is wearing a hat like hers, the other with her head slightly inclined and the other the dark brown of *her* dress and the other the blue of her eyes, and not one, not clear
not one, as far distant as I can see while they go past, is her.
all around me, *outside me*, above, there is a wonderful life that I may never have the strength to attain.
Here are the cold dews of September
Here is September with its flowers
   Its bracken dripping moist in the mist.

––––––––––

(late entry)
   '. . . This evening, I am thinking of her in such a vague and desparate way [so] that I can feel unable to breathe. These terrible [June evenings] 7 o'clock in the evening in June when I am shut up in a guard-room. This evening I shall go to Yarmouth or Plymouth by the sea shore beneath the great cloud-filled sky, in those little towns that are talked about in *David Copperfield*. I shall pass near the old dealer's booth, in front of the house with their little diamond window panes poor children will be playing and people will be sitting on their

212

doorsteps. [I shall pass along at nightfall, as of old, after dinner.]
A countryside [as I imagined it of old, imagined] which I
imagined after four o'clock when the summer evening stole
slowly over the apple-trees in the garden as far as the school
playground. I shall pass along there with my memories crushed
in my heart, for will [not] be perhaps further away from me
than on this present evening. And all this

I must revisit the scenes of the past alone

Without her thin, trailing dress, shadow leaning forward and
supported on my arm, a young woman with tears in her eyes

When shall I find again her gait and form of that afternoon as
she stood before me with her long brown costume and sunshade, it was for me the calm and the grace and the beauty of my
life — in a flash that recollection would rise up flooding my
heart like a very distant childhood memory.

1   The prototype of ardent lovers, Clitandre is a character in Molière's *Les
Femmes savantes*.

Appendix: III

Unpublished letter to Yvonne de Quiévrecourt, written by Fournier in Paris, September 1912, but not posted.

It is now more than seven years since you were lost to me. More than seven years have past since, one Whitsunday morning, you left me on the Pont des Invalides. You said 'We are two children, we have been foolish . . .'. And I could find no reply. In despair, yet resigned, I had been leaning against a pillar of the bridge. I watched you depart for ever. When you had crossed the quay, you hesitated before disappearing into the crowd, and looked towards me for a long time. Was it to say farewell or to give me to understand that I was not to follow you, or could it be that you had something to say to me? I have often wondered, but, doubtless, I shall never know.

Since then, I have never stopped searching for you. I have known for the last five years that you are married. How many nights of anguish, dark days, hopes, fits of despair, expectations, fine days, spent and wasted, are represented by what I am now telling you in a few brief dispassionate words. I have never passed a single week without walking along the Boulevard Saint Germain beneath the same windows at which you appeared several times during those all too brief days of summer 1905. One was the Saturday evening of a great downpour. Dressed in black, with a book in your hand, you raised the curtain and smiled to find me there . . . But never since that time has the curtain been raised again.

Nor have I failed to go to the Salon de la Nationale on each anniversary of our encounter. It was, you will remember, the first of June 1905, Ascension Day, between four and five o'clock? On each occasion I descend the great flight of stone steps where I looked at you for the first time; le Cours-la-

Reine. And, in despair, I repeat the boat trip which left me with such a wonderful memory to cherish.

I have forgotten nothing. I have remembered every minute of the short time when I have seen you in my life, every syllable of the few words you have spoken to me. These memories are all I have of you. I have kept them all, the humblest as well as the best. I recall, for example that [wall], Boulevard Saint Germain on which children had written something in chalk. You turned round to read it and glanced at me. But, among all other memories, I see with terrible clarity that moment of the same Thursday evening when, on the landing-stage of the Paris boat your lovely face was so close to mine, the face of the girl now lost to me. My eyes had taken their fill of your pure face until I was near to tears.

And do you imagine that I have been able to forget a single word of your long and only conversation on that Whitsunday morning? Ah! why did you say 'What's the use?' in such a calm but desperate way?

Now that I have found you again, I approach you with the same great (respect?), the same purity as of old. Do not ignore me cruelly as you did before when you saw me in front of the church of St Germain-des-Prés. Do you remember that you then recognized who I was? You allowed me to speak to you. For, it is something much more than love. Something more mysterious, purer. I say this with all the anguish of parting; it matters little now that you are married. Today I am burying this sorrow. But I cannot resign myself to not finding you again, to never setting eyes on you, spending my life in ignorance as to where you are. Am I to count only on death, who knows, to meet you again? I beg you to release me from this hell 'do not damn me by depriving me of your face'.[1]

I entreat you to pay heed to the dreadful thing I am saying to you with all my heart: it is this, away from your presence *I have no desire to live.*

Therefore I simply ask you this and nothing else. I am twenty-six, we are no longer children, I know what I am asking. Just this: to be no longer completely parted from you. You may command me to do what you like: to get married; to go far away. I will obey you. But, far away from you, I can write to you; near you, I can see you. That you can still grant

215

me; everything else you have taken from me.

Several of my old friends are naval officers, and I expect you know them. It will not be difficult for me to locate them. They will introduce me to you at your home. I am not asking for anything underhand, nothing that is not completely innocent. Only this: that at least you will not abandon me again as you did once, long ago, alone on a Paris bridge, without any hope of ever finding you again.

I beg you not to cast me into hell without giving deep thought to what you are going to decide . . .

1   Reference to Dante's *Inferno*.

Appendix: IV

Draft (with many erasures) of the letter written by Henri Fournier to Yvonne de Quiévrecourt after their meetings at Rochefort (23–25 May, 1913).

First I want to repeat to you what I whispered as you held out your hand to me at the moment when I left you . . .

'I leave in despair at having failed to make myself understood . . .'

Now, I am again far away from you in a small village in Normandy. It is the end of a sad summer morning. I am thinking of you whom I have at long last seen again. I think sometimes with joy, sometimes with bitterness of the friendship you have given me and with which I must needs learn to be satisfied.

I had come to you in such despair, in certain anticipation of the blow to my hopes, that at first your gesture of friendship filled me with joy. I had found you again. You did not rebuff me. You said: 'Yes, you may come . . . my husband will take you for a walk in the countryside that I love . . .'. I knew at least that I would not be losing you anymore. And I who had believed you lost to me for so long, was almost happy.

I was close to you. I could look at you. Sometimes your glance alighted on me. I was happy.

I rediscovered your graceful, unhurried movements, the way you gently inclined your head as you spoke, the purity of your face.

I loved your silences and I loved your words. They were always mysterious, prudent and wise beyond those of other women.

Waiting for you was a terrible agony. But hearing your steps along the path, feeling that it was you approaching in the shadow of the trees and pushing the open gate was more than I needed for my deepest joy.

Now I knew that all that had been given me for ever and that you would take it away from me. I knew that if one day I felt very unhappy, I could come and ask for it all again and that you would give me it again, since we were friends.

This is why I was so afraid of having upset you when I showed you the love-letter on Monday morning; and I very quickly told myself that I would no longer have the courage to write it now, so great would be my fear of losing the little I have.

And when you said to me: 'So, having come feeling ill, are you going to go away cured?' I replied 'yes', supposing that you were alluding to this awful journey, this distress, this headache.

At the time when you asked me this question, it is true that I felt reassured, appeased, happy again and I said so.

That was all I could say to you and all that I said. But if you could read what I wrote to my mother last night, you would realize that there is only one being in the whole world with whom I would have loved to spend my life. Once again I have seen the face of Beauty, purity and grace . . .

Index